RODNEY PEPPÉ'S

MOVING TOYS

RODNEY PEPPÉ'S

MOVING TOYS

 Sterling Publishing Co., Inc. New York

Published in 1980 by
Sterling Publishing Co., Inc.
Two Park Avenue
New York, N.Y. 10016

Paper ISBN: 0-8069-5424-8

Library ISBN: 0-8069-5423-X

Trade ISBN: 0-8069-5422-1

Published by arrangement with Evans Brothers, Ltd.
This edition available in the United States, Canada and the
Philippine Islands only

Printed in U.S.A.

CONTENTS

CONTENTS

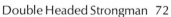

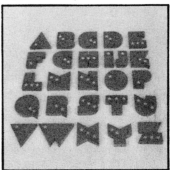

For Bill Janse

INTRODUCTION

The toys in this book were all made with the aid of a fretsaw machine (or jig saw, as it is termed in America). It is possible, however, to make the toys without a machine by using a hand fretsaw, holding the work flat on a table top, or by using a special model-making table with a cut-out V over which the work is placed for cutting, see page 3.

The book is not really intended for raw beginners, who would be entitled to a step-by-step analysis of each stage of construction. It is aimed, rather, at those who are fairly skilled but perhaps lack the designing ability to put their ideas into practice.

I was faced with the choice of excluding some of my favourite toys to accommodate instructional verbiage, or retaining them. I make no excuses for choosing the latter course. There are, nevertheless, some pieces which a ten-year-old could make, once the basic skill in using a fretsaw is mastered. So beginners, raw or otherwise, should not be deterred too much from the aims of this book. The degree of finish is, of course, reliant upon the expertise and talent of the individual, as with any craft.

It is, in the main, a source book of toy ideas from the past, redesigned for the present. A craftsman, looking at the pictorial information alone, should be able to make any toy, barely referring to the text. Generally speaking, anyone with a degree of skill, by using the text and pictures, should find the toys easy to make.

Antique toys have long held a fascination for me, especially ones that move with a simple mechanism. The Climbing Monkey who is seen actually to climb his string, possesses the most amusing and striking action of all the toys. His secret is clamped into an early tin toy at the beginning of this century . . . but all is revealed on page 50!

Perhaps the most intriguing mechanism, which shows Victorian ingenuity effectively, is the mysterious Sand Toy Leotard. This combines the principle of the hourglass with that of the mill wheel. What lends magic to the movement is that as the acrobat performs his antics, there is silence from the 'motor' – a sand motor concealed in the box.

Although the genesis of most of the toys is to be found in antique mechanisms there are exceptions, notably the Noah's Ark and the Two-Headed Strongman. The former has an assemble-it-yourself

1

rainbow concealed between its decks, perhaps reflecting modern packaging concepts; and the latter owes more to surrealism than to the Victorians.

The Circus Lion and Blinking Owl are toys made from my own illustrations for a children's book, but their mechanisms use old principles. The Owl's blink is achieved by using a lever movement designed by the great 19th-century toy book innovator Lothar Meggendorfer, whose paper engineering happily works in very thin plywood.

Where I had only pictorial reference for an old toy, I had to guess at the mechanism that moved it. The Musical Clown was a product of this guesswork, for I saw its ancestor in a book on automata, under the title of *Le Clown Orchestre*. There was nothing to show how it worked, and as I had never seen the actual toy I had to invent its workings.

I have endeavoured to cover most of the simple devices used in the past to activate movable toys but have purposefully omitted such favourites as the Jack-in-the-Box. Not because it is a toy that has endured to the present day, but because the doll inside the box is essentially three dimensional.

Most of the toys in this book are, if not two dimensional, fairly flat in design. This is partly because the thickness of the wood has governed the design of each toy, because they were made with a fretsaw. And it must not be supposed that the old craftsmen worked in this way. It is true that the Rocking Horse is three dimensional, but this has been achieved by sticking together three pieces of wood.

As a picture-book artist I have welcomed the fresh experience of working in polychromed wood and exploring playthings from the past. It is a journey I would not have undertaken unless I had been asked, and I am grateful to my publishers for inviting me and setting the wheels in motion. Those wheels have not stopped and I am still travelling. And learning.

TECHNIQUES

While maintaining that this is not so much a 'How to' as a 'What to' book, I must concede that I would be failing in my duty to the beginner, who, though warned, has nevertheless persisted. To those who know 'How to', please bear with me, or better still – start making a toy. Chapters on tools and materials follow.

Transferring the design on to wood

Depending on the complexity of the project, here are three ways:
1. Trace the design on to tracing paper with an HB pencil. Turn over the tracing paper so that the drawing is now facing the wood, and secure it with masking tape. You now rub down the design on to the wood with a burnisher, lifting the paper occasionally to check that the design has completely transferred.
2. Following the above method, transfer the design on to thin card instead of wood. Now cut out the outline so that you can use it as a template. Use a sharp 2H pencil for this, which will give a crisp line. You will find this method most useful for repeat work.
3. For a complicated pattern, or one which involves using the actual graphics, as in the Punch and Judy Show, you can make photocopies from this book. The procedure for colouring and transferring on to wood or card is dealt with in that chapter.

Whichever of the above methods you use, it should be remembered : the clearer your guide line, the more confident your cutting will be. Don't press too hard though, or you will bruise the wood.

Using the Fretsaw Machine

If a good quality blade is fitted and used correctly it should last, without breaking, until it is too blunt to continue. With trial and error you will find the particular stress limits for your machine and saw blades.

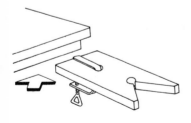

Fit blades with the teeth facing downwards, and, if you are using a hand fretsaw, cut only on the downward stroke.

Press down firmly, but not too hard, on the wood as you feed it through the blade, letting it find its own pace. Never force the wood through, so that it locks the blade, or you will eventually break it.

You can use all the teeth of the saw blade by varying the position of the saw table, up or down, as you feel the blade getting blunt.

For woodcutting saws the teeth are set wider apart than for metal cutting saws, the reason being that, as the wood has a grain, closely set teeth would tend to lock in the wood fibres. The choice of blade should be governed by the work, but it will be found that a medium blade will cope with most of the toys.

Draw with the saw

When you are cutting along a pencil line there is a tendency to waver if you don't concentrate. Think about what you are cutting. If it's a giraffe, don't slavishly follow the outline, *feel* the subtle curves of his long legs. Imagine stroking his back if you could. Identify with the work and you will achieve a smoother, more integrated result. Draw with the saw.

Cutting straight lines

You may prefer to follow a scored line rather than a pencil line when cutting long straight edges, for boxes perhaps.

Sand the edges at right-angles to the sanding block and any wavering in your cutting will disappear.

Cutting corners

If a really sharp angle is required, approach it from two directions, rather than turning at right-angles in the wood. Although this can be done in one continuous line, you may get unsightly scorch marks, which will show up on an unpainted toy.

To approach an angle from two directions, leave your cutting line and make a loop detour, so as to make a clear turn. For a continuous line, run the saw to the point where one line meets the other. Draw it back just about as much as its own thickness and slowly turn it till it faces in its new direction. This prevents locking and undue stress on the blade.

Cutting circles

Feed the work into the blade with a gradual circular motion, rather than as a series of straight lines, which by definition cannot exist on a circumference.

The slightest wavering will be apparent, and it must be said that it is not easy to cut a perfect circle . . . perhaps impossible. If a perfect circle is required, spin a second circle almost to the edge and sand away the irregularities.

Tools
Fretsaw machine
Drill stand
Electric drill
Vice
Twist drills
Countersinking and hole saw bits
Mole wrench
Wire cutters
Small pliers
Pin hammer
Needle files
Bradawl
Burnisher
Ratchet screwdriver
Electrical screwdriver
Tenon saw
Soldering iron
A pair of compasses with circle cutter
A pair of dividers
Metal rule 610mm (24in)
45° set square
Drawing pen and nibs such as Rotring Pen 0.3 and 0.6 nibs
HB and 2H pencils
Set of 4 sable brushes

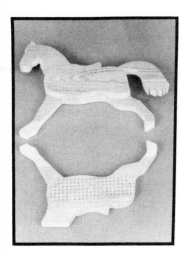

Cut in a good light

Always ensure that the shadow of your blade does not fall on the cutting line. It is hard enough to follow one line perfectly, let alone two! If you can face a window, so much the better.

Plural cutting

When two or more parts can be cut as one, this obviously makes life easier and the work more accurate. To cut exact duplicates or multiples, the best method is to rub down Polka dot adhesive (made by Letraset) which temporarily gives a firm binding and can be prized apart later, Fig. 1. The adhesive dots can be rubbed away with a ball of hardened rubber solution made from cow gum commonly known as 'cow rubber'.

Cutting interiors

To secure access to interior openings a small hole must be drilled to take the saw blade. When the interior is cut out, free the work from the blade and tighten up as usual.

Using a drill with a drill stand

Since it is all important to ensure that you are drilling at right-angles to the work surface, I recommend a power drill to be used with a drill stand. But a word of warning: check that the two fit together, as most manufacturer's accessories fit only their make of drill.

Drilling holes

When drilling through wood, always place another piece behind the hole to prevent splintering.

Fit the twist bit with a depth-stop if you are drilling to a fixed depth; or you can stick insulating tape round the bit to provide a guide. If you need to drill through a long piece of wood, sandwich the piece between two blocks of roughly the same height (to clear the chuck). The work is then kept in a vertical position to receive the drill bit accurately.

Always drill pilot holes before screwing, which will ensure the screw enters the work straight.

The ideal clearance hole for a number 8 gauge screw in softwood for example is 3mm ($\frac{3}{32}$in) and the pilot hole should be 2mm ($\frac{1}{16}$in). With hardwood the diameters are increased to 4mm ($\frac{5}{32}$in) and 3mm ($\frac{3}{32}$in) respectively.

The cutting guides
Black rectangles on the patterns denote the thickness of wood to be used. Numbers denote how many identical pieces are to be cut. Letters are used for identification purposes.

Generally speaking, cut on a continuous line but not on a dotted line. A continuous line will, however, sometimes carry the surface design; a dotted line will indicate variously a positioning of one piece on another, screw and string holes, or a partial cut.

Measurements
Metric and Imperial measurements have been given throughout. It must be emphasized that you should use either one scale or the other since the conversions are not exact.

MATERIALS

Softwood
This is timber from coniferous trees with needle-like leaves. I have used deal throughout which is sold for shelving. Splits in the boards, especially at the ends, are quite common and so are seal knots. Allowances should be made for these faults when buying timber, so it is always best to choose your own.

The thickness I have used throughout for softwood is 9mm ($\frac{3}{8}$in) and this was bought in widths of 144mm ($5\frac{5}{8}$in) and 93mm ($3\frac{11}{16}$in). These are the planed timber sizes, machined smooth for final cleaning up by you. That is to say: the original dimensions have been cut down to these finished sizes.

Plywood
This is made from an odd number of constructional veneers, bonded face to face, with the grain running in alternate directions. This helps to prevent warping by equalizing the tensions on the odd numbered veneers which range from 3-ply to 11-ply.

Lengths and widths of plywood are still mostly given in feet or inches by the trade and the thickness in millimetres (mm). Since we are dealing in small areas it is cheaper to buy 'off-cuts', and it is necessary only to know the thicknesses used in this book. They are: 6mm, 5mm, 4mm, and 1.5mm. This last one known as skin (Aero) ply may be a little difficult to find. Try model shops specializing in supplies for aeroplane or boat modellers.

Plywood is graded according to the outer veneers, but again, choose the boards yourself. Look for a close, even grain without blemish on what will be the outer surface of the toy. It won't matter if you have a small knot that doesn't show on the toy's interior, but beware of hollow areas between the veneers. This you can easily check by looking along the edges of the board. Birch plywood has been used for many of the toys.

Abrasive papers
Three grades of glass-paper (commonly known as sandpaper) are needed: coarse, medium and fine. The procedure is to work through the grades until the required degree of finish is achieved. Garnet-paper lasts longer than glass-paper and gives a cleaner cut but is sometimes difficult to obtain. Silicone-carbide paper, better known as 'wet-and-dry', is used like the other papers when dry. Emery paper is unsuitable, being for metal finishing only.

When sanding a comparatively large flat area, wrap the abrasive paper around a flat cork block, or lay the paper on a flat cork surface. Always keep the abrasive paper in a straight line with the direction of the grain, whichever method you employ. If you sand across the grain, scratches will appear which are tedious to remove.

Primer
The first coat of paint on new work is a primer and should not be confused with an undercoat, which helps to cover previous coats. The primer seals the surface and is especially useful in preventing oil-based paints from sinking into it.

Since I have mainly applied water-based paints, a coat of white emulsion has only occasionally been used as a primer. My own preference is usually to omit it in favour of an extra coat of the top colour, which may horrify some experts. I do, however, seal the surface by spraying on a light coat of polyurethane lacquer which, when dry, allows me to paint directly on to it. In this way I can leave unpainted areas, such as a face, allowing the wood colour and grain to show through. I am then free to paint in the face details, without fear of the wet paint soaking into the surface.

The lacquer primer is to seal the surface only, so be careful not to overdo the spraying or you will find difficulty in getting the wet paint to take on a glossy surface. If you do find the paint retracting as you apply it, rub some spittle on to the wood to 'key' the surface. Rude, but effective.

Sometimes the opacity of a white emulsion paint can mar the attractive relationship which exists between wood and paint, and this method of applying a lacquer primer gets over the problem nicely. There are times, though, when the emulsion primer really comes into its own, particularly when repaired areas have to be covered.

Fillers
If you make a mistake in drilling, or the grain of the plywood is too coarse, it will be necessary to use fillers to rectify these faults.

Where you wish to re-drill a hole, almost on the same spot, you can use plastic padding. If you wish to smooth the surface of a board, you can apply plastic wood with a palette knife, or use a grain filler liberally. When dry and thoroughly hard, sand lightly with the grain.

Adhesives
A woodworking adhesive such as Evo-stick has been used throughout, giving way, in very special cases, to an instant adhesive which bonds skin to skin in seconds such as Loctite Super Glue-3. Children should not use it.

For boxes a strong wallpaper adhesive has been employed in sticking lining paper to plywood and decorative papers over the lining papers.

Brushes
As a matter of personal preference, I like using short-haired sables, series 7 from Winsor & Newton, sizes 000 and 00 for very fine work.

For general purpose painting or varnishing, the shape and size of brush is again a matter of choice. But stick to sables for the best results.

Paint

Plaka colour, made by Pelican, has largely been used throughout. It is a quick-drying casein emulsion with a velvety, matt sheen. All shades have a good light fastness, the great advantage being that the paint becomes smudge-proof on drying, and waterproof in about twenty-four hours.

In applying Plaka colour, don't work too thickly. Impasto and brush marks are fine in a painting but on a toy they look clumsy. It is better to work wet since the paint has a very good covering capacity. Paint two coats or more if you need to.

Enamel paint such as that made by Humbrol is oil-based, and has been used to a lesser degree than Plaka. It has the advantage of providing its own built-in gloss finish, thus rendering the application of a lacquer unnecessary. Its disadvantage is that it is difficult to work in fine detail, and takes longer to dry.

Polyurethane Lacquer

This is used as a final clear gloss finish for all items except the enamel painted objects. The lacquer has the effect of darkening yet enhancing the matt colours, and protects the toys with a durable covering.

It can be applied as a spray, or with a brush from a tin. Pieces such as the Bird Tree or Goldilocks and the Three Bears are best sprayed, but be careful not to miss the edges which will need more lacquer since they are more absorbent. Touch up with a brush if necessary.

With brush application, especially on unpainted wood, lay the first coat across the grain and finish off by brushing out with the grain.

Whether you use a brush or spray it will be necessary to have a lacquering board. This can be a piece of plywood, say 305mm x 254mm (12in x 10in) with little blocks, about 6mm ($\frac{1}{4}$in) high, irregular lengths, spaced at intervals to support the pieces to be lacquered, so that they don't stick to the board. Don't load on too much lacquer or this will run making an unsightly ridge on the underside of the piece, which in its turn you may wish to lacquer.

Allow the work to dry, overnight if possible, in a warm temperature. You can speed things up a little by placing the lacquering board on a central heating boiler, but experiment first.

When dry, lightly sand with fine dry abrasive paper before applying a second coat of lacquer. The final coat should also be sanded to remove high spots, then rubbed down with the grain. Not all the toys will need this degree of finish, though.

Two pitfalls to watch for:
1. Don't apply a second coat too soon, or you may find that the first coat cockles and unpleasant wrinkling results.
2. Always ensure that the lacquer will not act as a solvent upon an oil-based printing colour. Always test, if you are unsure how agents will react to the lacquer.

Cleaning Brushes
If Plaka colour has been used, wash brushes out with soap and luke-warm water. For polyurethane lacquer and enamel paints, soak the brushes in white spirit, or lighter fuel. Squeeze out with a rag or toilet paper. Repeat until the paint or varnish has disappeared, and finally wash out with soap and water. But you need not wash each time; only when you have finished lacquering for the day.

Screws

Countersunk screws are used throughout, mostly brass No. 8s or No. 6s. Where a screw length is unobtainable, use a longer screw and nip off the end to the correct length.

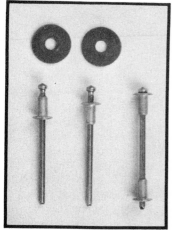

Panel Pins
These steel pins which are tapped in with a pin hammer are invaluable for holding together the sides of boxes when gluing. I have used 12mm ($\frac{1}{2}$in) pins and nipped off the ends (at an angle to keep a point), when they are too long for the work, which isn't often.

Pop Rivets
These have not been used for their intended purpose but serve as good fixings when adapted. The adaptation being that the rivet head is inverted, allowing the pin to pass through the work with a stop either end, Fig. 1. The projecting end is then pinched with a mole wrench, thus locking the pin.

BALANCING TOYS

ROCKING HORSE

This is based on a 19th-century watercolour, but it is not supposed to be an accurate representation of an old rocking horse. The trimmings are bits of modern haberdashery giving a decorative effect. It's a shelf piece rather than a toy.

Cut from 10mm ($\frac{3}{8}$in) softwood

The horse is simply made from three sections, which can be seen on page 5. After gluing the sections together, it is largely a question of shaping the horse's neck, with an abrasive paper.

The horse's hooves are glued to the rocker boards. These are cut from 4mm ($\frac{1}{6}$in) plywood and glued to the rockers.

The stirrups are made from soldering wire which can be pinched at the base with pliers. The saddle is a piece of suede and the girth is made from coloured felt. The brasses are punched from metallic gold card.

When painting, try to get the dappled grey effect by applying a grey base over a white emulsion primer. Then sand it down. Paint white spots of varying sizes.

Materials

Softwood
210 x 340 x 10mm
$8\frac{1}{4}$ x $13\frac{1}{2}$ x $\frac{3}{8}$in

Plywood
60 x 50 x 4mm
$2\frac{1}{2}$ x 2 x $\frac{1}{6}$in

Soldering wire

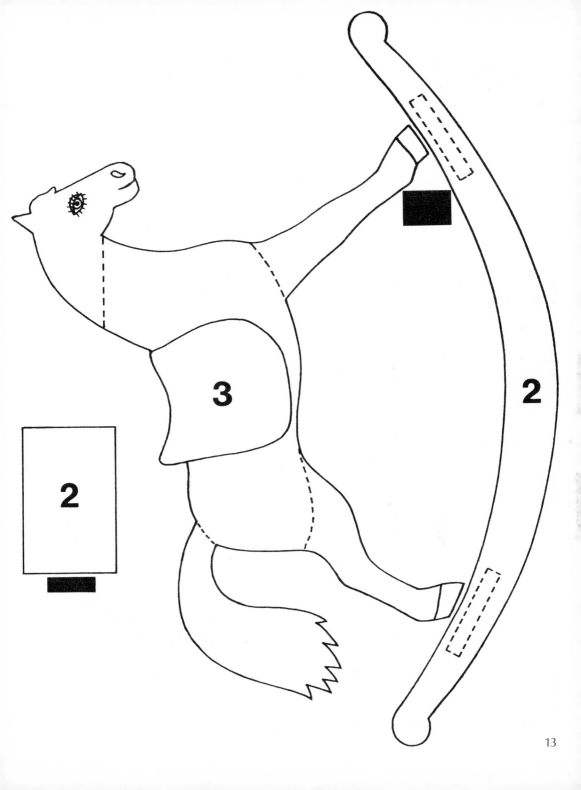

3

2

2

13

BALANCING TUMBLERS

The ancestor of this toy was made from metal rods and featured solid, three dimensional clowns. I have redesigned it for the fretsaw as a very simple but effective toy to make.

The running time is forty seconds – that is the time it takes the tumblers to reach the bottom of the frame. It's a very pretty action to watch, as they rotate gently forwards and then backwards to their destination.

Cut from 4mm ($\frac{1}{6}$in) plywood
Cut two frames and drill three 6mm ($\frac{1}{4}$in) holes into the base of each. Cut three 6mm ($\frac{1}{4}$in) dowels 95mm (3$\frac{3}{4}$in) long. Glue them into the holes to join the frames.

(handwritten margin note:
3 $\frac{3}{4}$ 3 $\frac{12}{16}$
- 5/16   - 5/16
3 $\frac{7}{16}$ Length
between frames.)

Cut from 1.5mm ($\frac{1}{16}$in) skin (Aero) ply
Plural cut four tumblers (see Techniques, page 5). Drill 3mm ($\frac{1}{8}$in) hole through them.

Cut from 10mm ($\frac{3}{8}$in) softwood
Cut one piece A and two pieces B. Drill a central 6mm ($\frac{1}{4}$in) hole through central pivot A. Drill 3mm ($\frac{1}{8}$in) hole through the cross section along dotted line. Drill two 3mm ($\frac{1}{8}$in) holes into outer pivots B, one through the cross-bar and the other to a depth of 10mm ($\frac{3}{8}$in) as the dotted line shows.

6mm ($\frac{1}{4}$in) and 3mm ($\frac{3}{8}$in) dowels
(handwritten: $\frac{1}{8}$")

Cut 6mm ($\frac{1}{4}$in) dowel 145mm (5$\frac{3}{4}$in) long tapering the ends slightly. Cut two 3mm ($\frac{1}{8}$in) dowels 55mm (2$\frac{1}{4}$in) long. Cut two 3mm ($\frac{1}{8}$in) dowels 35mm (1$\frac{3}{8}$in) long.

Glue pivot A to the centre of the 145mm (5$\frac{3}{4}$in) long 6mm ($\frac{1}{4}$in) dowel. Glue the two 55mm (2$\frac{1}{4}$in) long 3mm ($\frac{1}{8}$in) dowels into the upright sections of pivots B and either side of the cross section in pivot A. See Fig. 1.

Pass the two 3mm ($\frac{1}{8}$in) dowels 35mm (1$\frac{3}{8}$in) long, through the cross sections of pivots B. This leaves 3mm ($\frac{1}{8}$in) projections on to which each tumbler is fixed. Test the movement first, and when satisfied paint the toy. When lacquering, leave the track (that is the top edges of the frame where the bar rolls) and the cross-bar matt. This ensures a good grip.

Materials

Plywood
340 x 160 x 4mm
13 x 6$\frac{1}{2}$ x $\frac{1}{6}$in

Softwood
115 x 40 x 10mm
4 x 1$\frac{1}{2}$ x $\frac{3}{8}$in

Skin Plywood
160 x 100 x 1.5mm
6$\frac{1}{2}$ x 4 x $\frac{1}{16}$in

Dowel
430 x 6mm
17 x $\frac{1}{4}$in

185 x 3mm
7$\frac{1}{4}$ x $\frac{1}{8}$in

Metallic card

Now fix the tumblers on to their pivots by gluing a small disc punched from metallic card to each projection.

Ensure that they move freely on their pivots, and they are ready to roll!

5/16

Fig.1

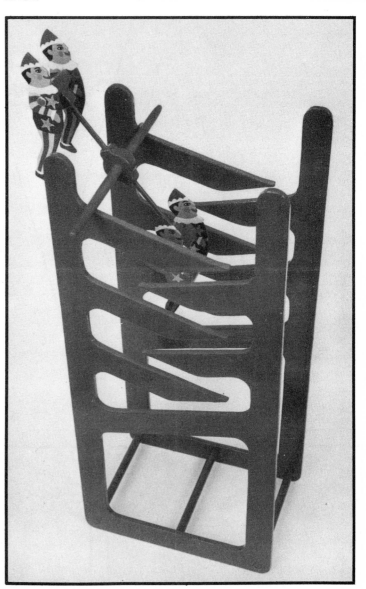

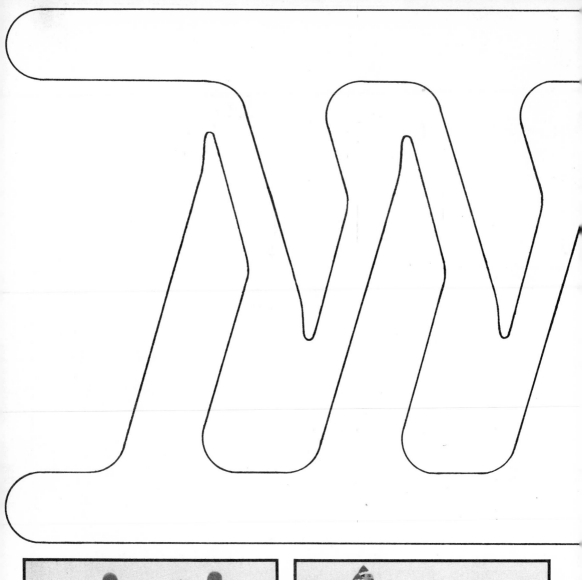

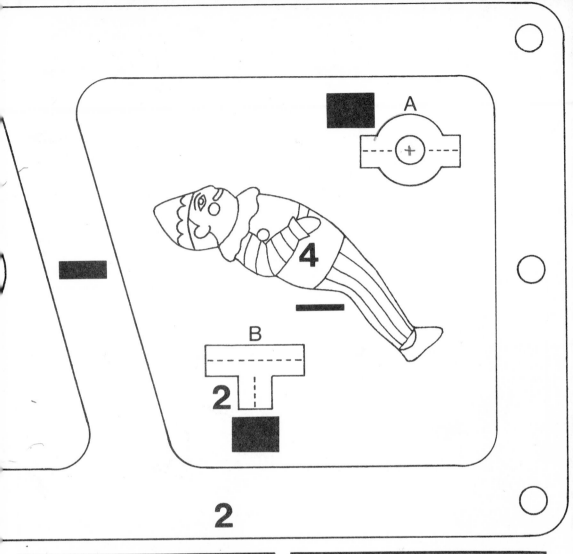

A

B

4

2

2

SAND-TOY 'LEOTARD'

This is my favourite toy and one that intrigued little Victorians. The fascination lies in the near magical machinery that works the acrobat. In the back of the box there is some silver sand in the base. When the box is turned over slowly to the right the sand gathers on to a V-shaped shelf at the top of the box and then trickles through a hole on to a small replica of a watermill wheel. This is attached to a spindle and activates 'Leotard'. (J. Leotard invented the flying trapeze in 1859). Being jointed at the limbs and neck enables him to perform innumerable and intricate movements in an unpredictable sequence.

The Box – cut from 4mm ($\frac{1}{6}$in) plywood

Cut two sides 224mm x 75mm ($8\frac{13}{16}$in x 3in). Cut the top and base 150mm x 75mm ($5\frac{15}{16}$in x 3in). Cut a front panel 224mm x 145mm ($8\frac{13}{16}$in x $5\frac{11}{16}$in) as shown on the cutting guide. Drill 2mm ($\frac{1}{16}$in) hole in it. Decorate the front panel with a picture of the circus or a circus bill. You might consider a simpler but effective approach by using a matt black background for the brightly coloured acrobat.

Fig. 1

Materials

Plywood
325 x 480 x 4mm
13 x 19 x $\frac{1}{6}$in

Skin (Aero) Ply
75 x 40 x 1.5mm
3 x 1$\frac{1}{2}$ x $\frac{1}{16}$in

Tin
75 x 75mm
3 x 3in

Piano wire
64 x 2mm
2$\frac{1}{2}$ x $\frac{1}{16}$in

Pliable Wire
40mm
1$\frac{1}{2}$in

Card
140 x 50 x 2mm
5$\frac{1}{2}$ x 2 x $\frac{1}{16}$in

Thin Card
190 x 75mm
7$\frac{1}{2}$ x 3in

Glue and pin the outer frame positioning the front panel inside 30mm (1⅛in) from the front edge. Seal the inside edges with masking tape so that sand cannot escape. Cut a back panel 232mm x 153mm (9⅛in x 6in).

The Sand Motor

Cut out two discs D from thin cardboard. Drill 2mm ($\frac{1}{16}$in) hole at the centre. Cut four sections E and fold by scoring along the centres. Glue the sections to the discs. Pass 2mm ($\frac{1}{16}$in) piano wire 64mm (2½in) long through the discs so that 10mm (⅜in) protrudes at one end and 30mm (1⅛in) at the other. This is the spindle. See Fig. 1.

Use pliable wire 40mm (1½in) long to anchor the spindle to the top disc. Do this by soldering one end of the wire to the spindle – if you have a soldering iron – if not, use strong glue. Fit the other end into 6mm (¼in) cut you make in the outer disc edge. Bend it over and clamp under.

Make a counterweight of solder or lead shot (fishing tackle). Fix it on to the outer disc in the six o'clock position. This weight counterbalances the acrobat so when you have made him you must test their compatability.

Cut out the V-shaped shelf A from 2mm ($\frac{1}{16}$in) card. Scoring along the dotted line. Punch or drill a 2mm ($\frac{1}{16}$in) hole.

Cut from thin tin sheet, pieces B, C and G. Drill 2mm ($\frac{1}{16}$in) holes and smooth off the rough edges.

Fig. 2

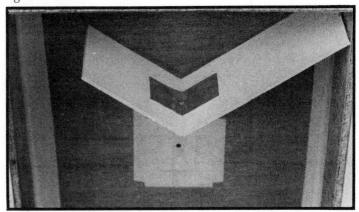

Materials

Silver sand
Masking tape
1 lead weight
2 ball-headed pins
1 washer

Bend the shelf card A to the correct angle and likewise the tin piece C. Glue them together so that the holes register. Stick the assembled shelf to the back of the front panel.

Glue and tape in position tin piece B registering with the hole in the front panel, Fig. 2.

Leotard – cut from 1.5mm ($\frac{1}{16}$in) skin (Aero) ply

Drill or pierce very small holes to take pins through the neck, limbs and body. F is sandwiched and glued between the two outer halves of the body. The neck fits into the recess between

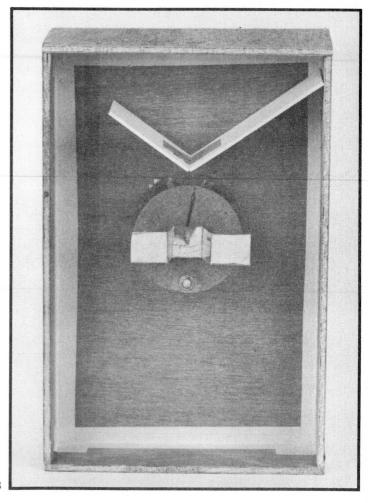

Fig. 3

them. Use ball-headed pins, cut to length, to lock the pins on the outside. Either solder blobs on to the ends or bend them over to act as stops for the inside.

Assembly

Place a washer on the spindle to separate the inner disc from the front panel. Insert the spindle so that 25mm (1in) protrudes through to the front of the box.

Bend the tin piece G into shape to act as a socket for the spindle, Fig. 3. Glue this in position on the back panel so that when the box is sealed the wheel runs freely. Fill the base of the box with about 50mm (2in) of silver sand.

Place the back over the frame, fitting the spindle into G. Make sand tests by temporarily sealing the back panel with masking tape and turning the box slowly twice to the right. Attach the figure to the spindle protruding in the front. When you are satisfied that the counterweight compensates Leotard, glue and pin on the back panel.

Cover the box with lining paper using a strong wallpaper adhesive and when dry cover that with a decorative paper.

Temporarily fix Leotard to his bar through the holes in his hands. Now comes the final test before you fix him forever in position. Ensure that you get the best 'performance' – that is an unpredictable pattern of movements rather than just forward somersaults. Explore his talents and when the best position is found, secure him firmly to the bar by means of solder or very strong instant adhesive.

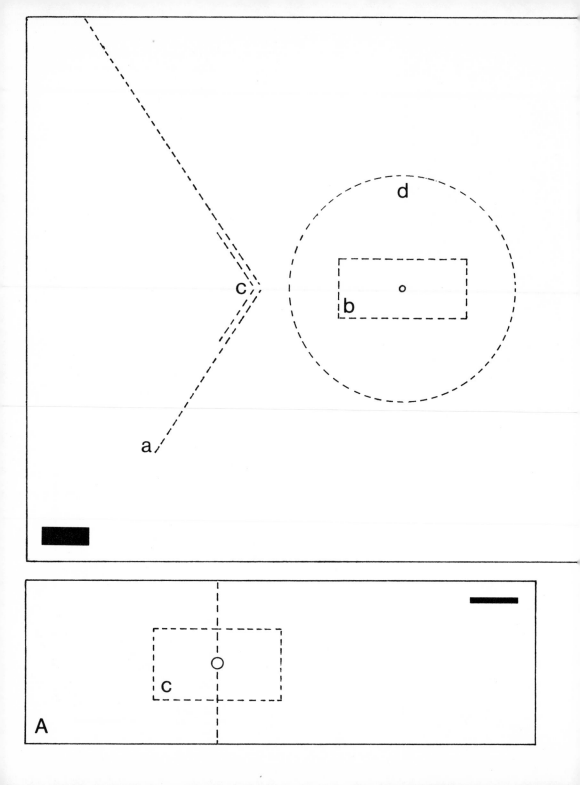

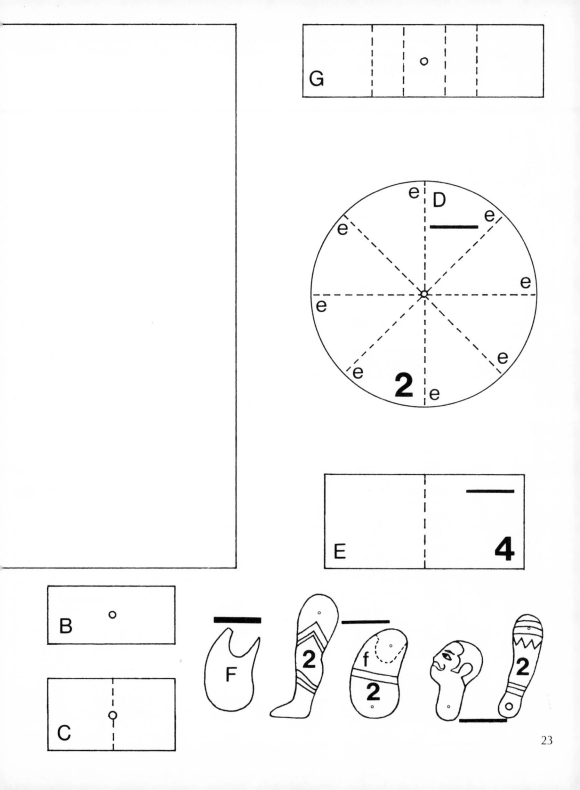

G

D

2

E   4

B

C

F   2   2   2

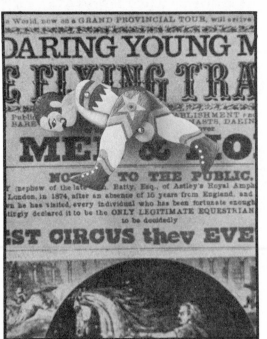

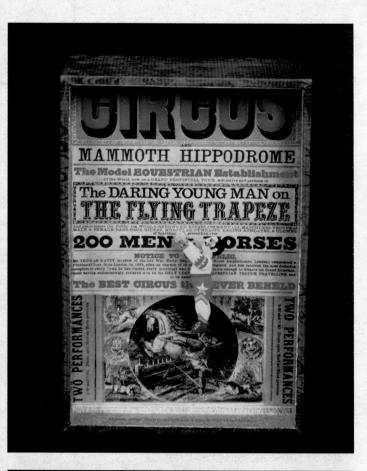

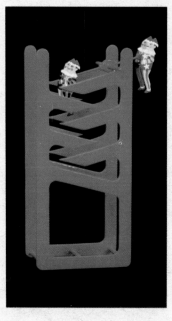

(Top Left) Sand Toy 'Leotard'
(Above) Balancing Tumblers
(Left) Rocking Horse

(Below) Torsion Toy Acrobat
      (detail)

(Bottom) Hand-wound
      Drummer (detail)

(Right) The Tivoli Acrobats

THE TIVOLI ACROBATS

. . . so called, because they are based on a Victorian game of that name. Their appeal, especially to very young children, lies in the ability of the acrobats to act as a team. Feed a ball into the top clown's cup and its weight transfers the ball into the next cup. While the first clown counterbalances backwards, the second passes the ball to the third who repeats the operation; and the fourth clown drops the ball on to the bell which gives out a satisfying 'ting'. The ball then rolls on to the board and one scores as in a game of Bagatelle.

Cut from 4mm ($\frac{1}{6}$in) plywood

The cutting guide for the box lid, sides, back and front has been drawn half size, so double up on all the box measurements. The numerals can be photocopied, cut out and used in conjunction with the base-board.

Drill clearance holes for No. 6 screws in the box sides at E. Drill 2mm ($\frac{1}{16}$in) hole for the support arm in one of the sides at C and likewise into the corresponding side of the lid D. Drill a pilot hole for the bell at F and four pilot holes for No. 8 screws to hold the acrobats. Drill four 2mm ($\frac{1}{16}$in) holes for pop rivet pins at their feet.

Cut the base 605mm x 240mm (23$\frac{7}{8}$in) x 9$\frac{1}{2}$in). Glue and pin the box sides, the front and back to the base.

Fit the lid of the box with 12mm ($\frac{1}{2}$in) cushion picture frame moulding G, glued and pinned along the width at the bottom. Drill pilot holes for No. 6 screws 20mm ($\frac{3}{4}$in) long into the ends of the moulding at E.

First line the outside of the box and then cover with a decorative paper. Ensure that you do not lose the positions of holes drilled in the lid for you should now cover the inside of the lid with thin coloured card. To keep the holes located, pierce a pin through the paper.

Plural cut two sets of acrobats (see Techniques, page 5). Drill wide clearance holes for No. 8 screws through all four of them. Prime and paint them in pairs.

Cut four 16mm ($\frac{5}{8}$in) dowels F into 12mm ($\frac{1}{2}$in) lengths. Drill wide clearance holes through them for No. 8 screws 22mm ($\frac{7}{8}$in) long.

Fix 25mm (1in) vessel heads (plastic cups available from model makers shops) to the hands by drilling clearance and pilot holes

Materials

Plywood
605 x 550 x 4mm
24 x 22 x $\frac{1}{6}$in

Cushion Picture Frame
Moulding
240mm
10in

Dowel
50 x 16mm
2 x $\frac{5}{8}$in

2 No.6 screws
4 No.8 screws
Bicycle bell top

4 pop rivet pins

4 x 25mm (1in) plastic cups
4 miniature screws
4 lead weights

Square Battening
560 x 6mm
22 x $\frac{1}{4}$in

for miniature screws. Wooden balls 20mm ($\frac{3}{4}$in) in diameter to fit the cups should be coloured by dropping into coloured inks.

Counterweight the backs of the acrobats with lead fishing tackle against the weight of the wooden balls. Squeeze the lead flat with a mole wrench and glue into position. Trial and error will find the correct balance for each acrobat, tipping over when the ball is in the cup and returning to the vertical when empty. Insert four pop rivet pins in front of each acrobat's leg as indicated.

Cut 2mm ($\frac{1}{16}$in) 6 sheet mounting board to fit over the base. Cut the required apertures in this base-board and fix photocopies of the numerals, covered with transparent sticky coloured film underneath.

Use 6mm (¼in) square battening to produce the fences A and B. Stick them to the base-board as indicated. Use battening under the board to provide the necessary rake to allow the balls to move forward. Glue in position.

Cut 2mm ($\frac{1}{16}$in) piano wire 180mm (7in) long for the support arm. Bend it into a U and L shape at the ends to fit into holes c and d.

Fix a small bicycle bell top into F, and the acrobats are ready to play.

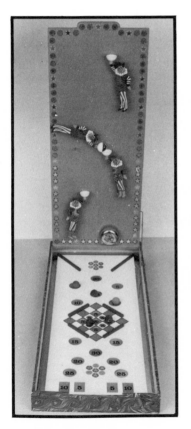

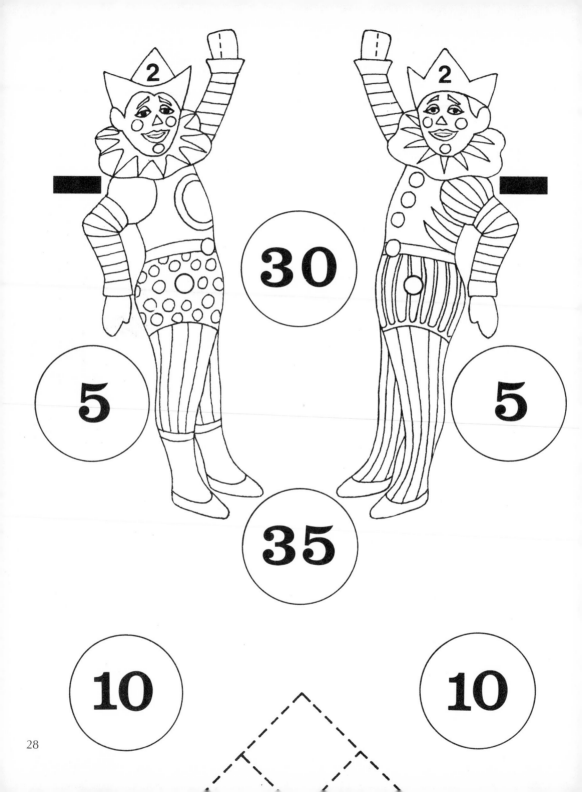

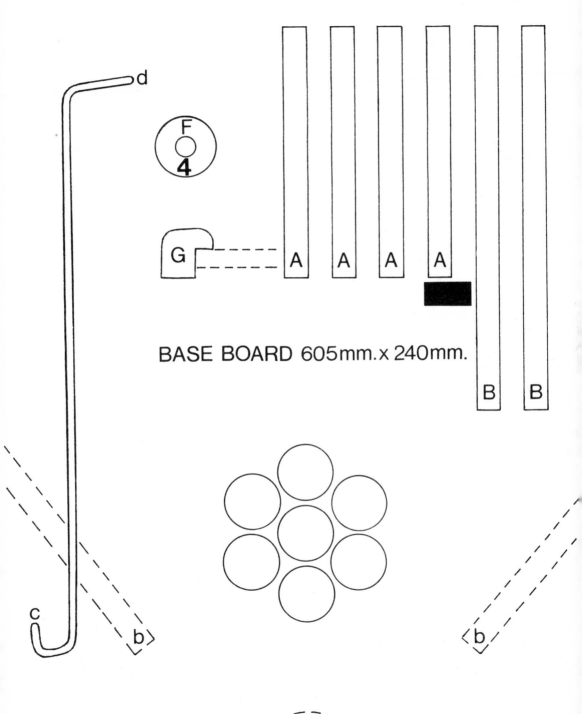

BASE BOARD 605mm. x 240mm.

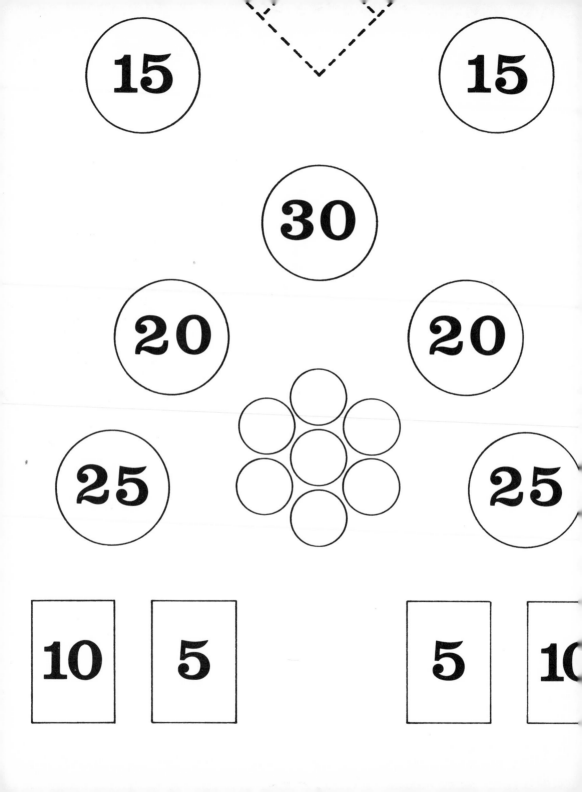

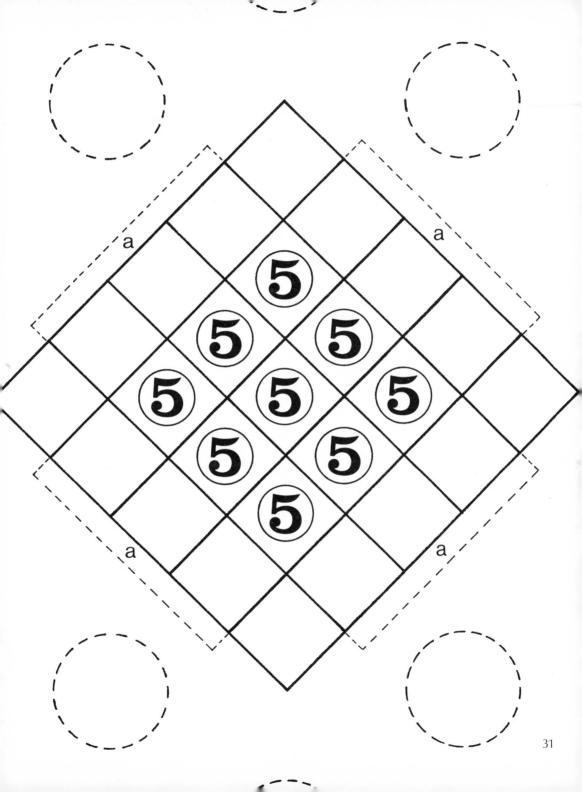

a

a

a

a

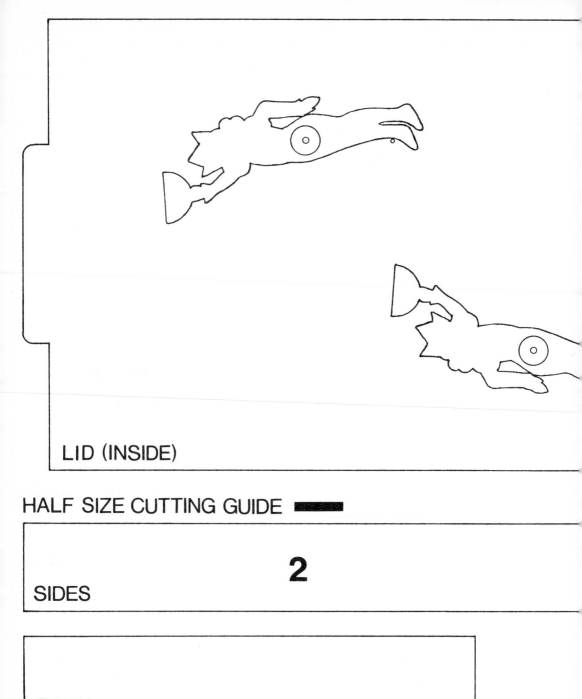

LID (INSIDE)

HALF SIZE CUTTING GUIDE ▬

2

SIDES

BACK

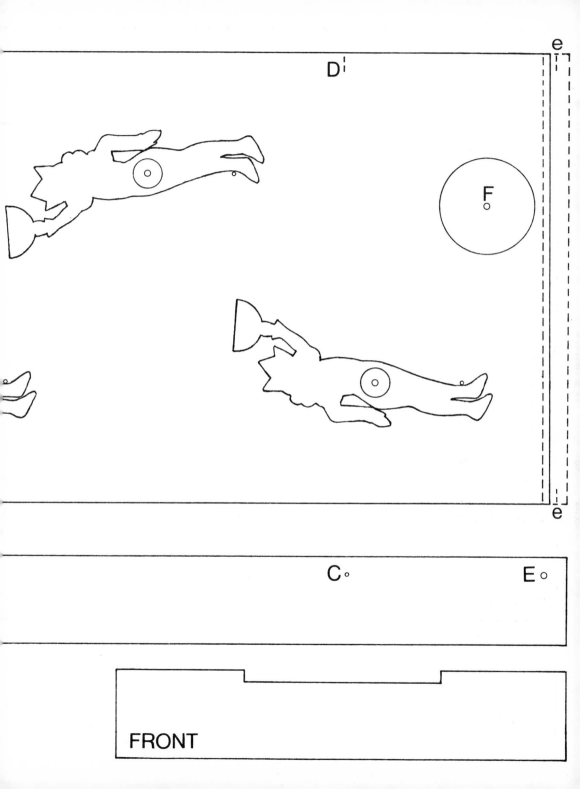

D

e

F

e

C

E

FRONT

STRING TOYS

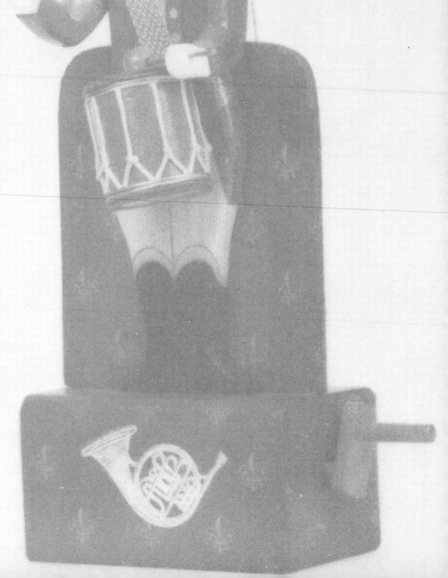

TORSION TOY ACROBAT

Most children have had a torsion toy at some time, and its popularity through the ages is doubtless based upon the feeling of complete control one has over the actions. The pressure applied to the base of the sticks stretches the twisted string so as to make the acrobat somersault at will and even stop in mid air.

Cut from 4mm ($\frac{1}{6}$in) plywood
Plural cut the arms and legs (see Techniques, page 5). Drill 3mm ($\frac{1}{8}$in) holes for pop rivets in the shoulders and thighs. Drill two 2mm ($\frac{1}{16}$in) holes through the hands. Drill a 2mm ($\frac{1}{16}$in) hole in the neck. Drill 3mm ($\frac{1}{8}$in) hole through the two body halves.

Cut from 1.5mm ($\frac{1}{16}$in) skin (Aero) ply
Plural cut body pieces and drill a 2mm ($\frac{1}{16}$in) hole at neck. Glue piece A between the two body halves. Sand and shape the pieces rounding the edges slightly.

Prime and paint the acrobat and decorate him with silver stars. Fix the arms and head to the body by means of a pop rivet pin, two washers, and two inverted rivet heads to act as stops. Do likewise for the legs. Cut the pins to length and in so doing this should lock the pins. See Techniques, page 10.

Cut from 10mm ($\frac{3}{8}$in) softwood
Cut out pieces for the frame and drill four 3mm ($\frac{1}{8}$in) holes through each side piece. Drill 3mm ($\frac{1}{8}$in) holes to a depth of 12mm ($\frac{1}{2}$in) in the ends of the cross-piece. Use four No. 6 screws to put the frame together. Pass string through the top two holes one side of the frame, cross before passing through acrobat's hands and cross again before passing through frame to tie.

Materials

Plywood
155 x 230 x 4mm
6 x 9 x $\frac{1}{6}$in

Skin (Aero) Ply
100 x 70 x 1.5mm
4 x 3 x $\frac{1}{16}$in

Softwood
305 x 80 x 10mm
12 x 3 x $\frac{3}{8}$in

2 pop rivets
2 extra rivet heads
2 washers
4 No.6 screws

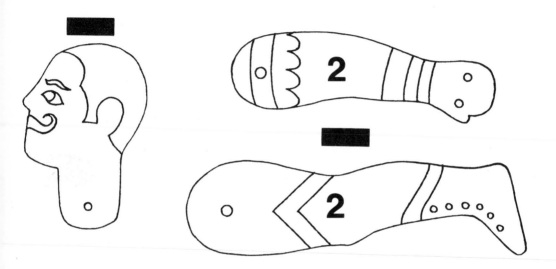

2

2

2

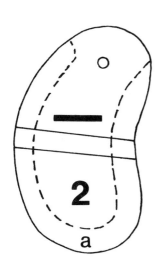

a

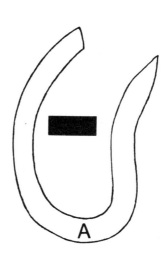

A

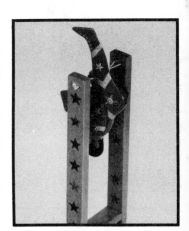

HAND-WOUND DRUMMER

In the 1820s, toys with very simple hand-wound movements were being sold in London. One shop which sold such toys was called Edlin's Rational Repository of Amusement and Instruction! The mechanism of the Edlin dolls is used for this toy. A wooden crank handle turns a roller concealed in the platform base. This winds two separate strings simultaneously, but in alternating rhythm.

Cut from 10mm ($\frac{3}{8}$in) softwood

Cut out body, arms and support block B. Drill pilot holes in the figure at the dotted lines, for No. 6 screws 20mm ($\frac{3}{4}$in) long. Drill clearance holes in the upper arms. Drill 2mm ($\frac{1}{16}$in) holes in the hands to take pop rivet pins, angled towards the body. Drill three pilot holes in the support block B for No. 6 screws.

Cut from 4mm ($\frac{1}{6}$in) plywood

Cut out the remaining pieces. Drill 6mm ($\frac{1}{4}$in) holes in the sides D. Glue and pin the front and back of the platform base C to the sides D. Drill three clearance holes for No. 6 screws through the top E. Drill two further 10mm ($\frac{3}{8}$in) holes through E, for strings. Glue and pin E to sides D and E.

Drill three clearance holes for No. 6 screws through the back-board F. Glue and pin the support block B centrally, flush with the base of the back-board F.

Cover the platform base and the back-board and support separately, with a military style printed paper. Screw the back-board F into position on to the platform E from underneath.

Paint and decorate the figure. To make the drum, use a stiff cardboard roll, 28mm ($1\frac{1}{8}$in) diameter by 35mm ($1\frac{3}{8}$in) deep. Cut out tin circles from a biscuit tin with strong scissors. Cover with edging material and string.

Screw the completed figure to the back-board with No. 6 screws 10mm ($\frac{3}{8}$in) long. Fix the arms loosely with No. 6 screws 20mm ($\frac{3}{4}$in) long and paint the screw heads. Screw two small screw eyes into the back of the shoulders. Insert two pop rivet pins 45mm ($1\frac{3}{4}$in) long, through the hands, and fix two 10mm ($\frac{3}{8}$in) wooden beads to complete the drum sticks.

Materials

Softwood
100 x 200 x 10mm
4 x 8 x $\frac{3}{8}$in

Plywood
200 x 200 x 4mm
8 x 8 x $\frac{1}{16}$in

Dowel
75 x 20mm
3 x $\frac{3}{4}$in

75 x 5mm
3 x $\frac{3}{16}$in

2 beads
2 No.6 screws 10mm ($\frac{3}{8}$in) long
cardboard roll 28mm ($1\frac{1}{8}$in) diameter
2 No.6 screws 20mm ($\frac{3}{4}$in) long
2 small screw eyes
tin sheet
2 pop rivet pins

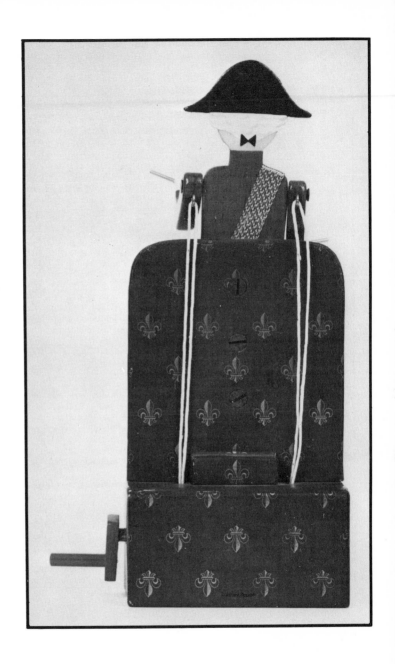

2   C

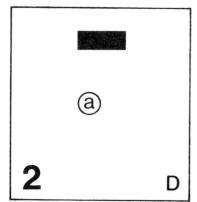

ⓐ

2   D

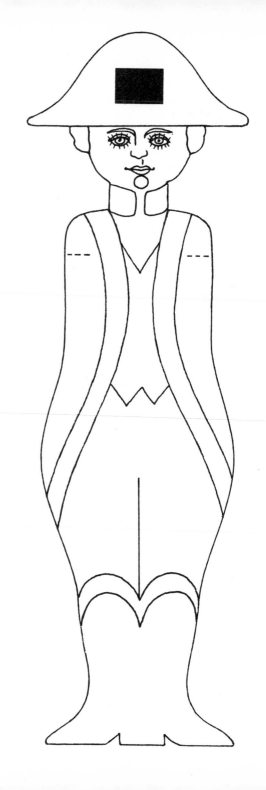

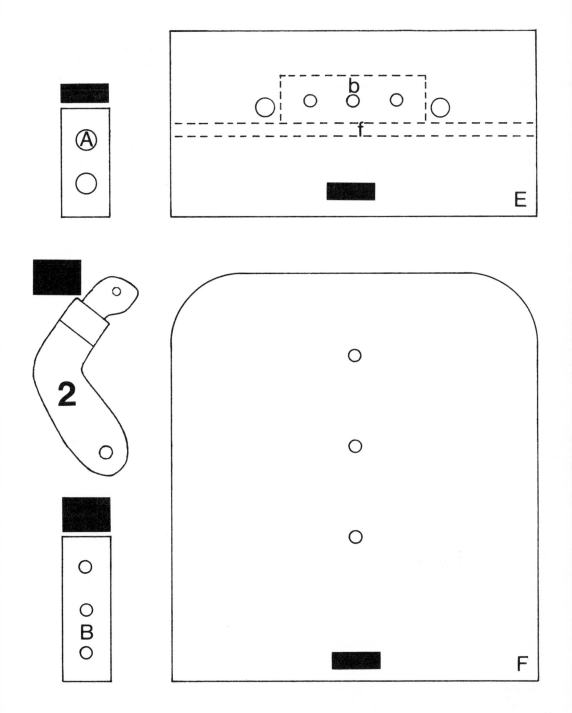

A

2

B

E

b

f

F

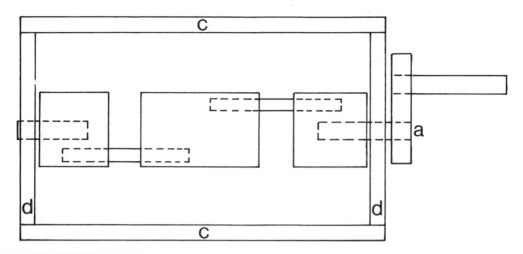

The Edlin Roller

Cut 20mm ($\frac{3}{4}$in) dowel into two 20mm ($\frac{3}{4}$in) lengths and one 32mm ($1\frac{1}{4}$in) length. Drill two central 6mm ($\frac{1}{4}$in) holes to a depth of 12mm ($\frac{1}{2}$in) into the former adding two off-centre 3mm ($\frac{1}{8}$in) holes at opposite ends. Drill two off-centre 3mm ($\frac{1}{8}$in) holes into the longer, middle dowel, to a depth of 12mm ($\frac{1}{2}$in) at opposite ends.

Cut 5mm ($\frac{3}{16}$in) dowels into lengths of 20mm ($\frac{3}{4}$in), 25mm (1in) and 30mm ($1\frac{3}{16}$in). These are the two central dowel pins and the handle. (Rub some wax into the holes a in the sides D to ease the friction.) Assemble and glue the dowels as in the diagram using two 3mm ($\frac{1}{8}$in) dowels 35mm ($1\frac{3}{8}$in) long.

Two pieces of string are fed through the arm hooks and the two holes in the top E. Tie the ends around the 3mm ($\frac{1}{8}$in) dowel pins, between the rollers. Turn the handle and the drummer will beat the drum which is glued to the body so that he plays a tinny tune.

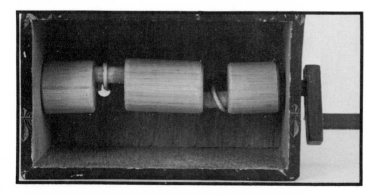

THE BLINKING OWL

This is my homage to the 19th-century innovator of toy books, Lothar Meggendorfer. The blink mechanism is adapted from one of his movable books worked by card levers. But the Owl is based upon one of my own children's book illustrations.

The mechanics of the blink are remarkably life-like. On pulling out the tab the Owl doesn't merely shut his eyes and then open them on the return of the tab. He blinks : open-shut-open, in one pull, or push of the lever. He flaps his wings and tail at the same time, for good measure.

Paint all parts and test the movements before sticking down.

Cut from 5mm ($\frac{3}{16}$in) plywood

Cut out the eye holes from the background F. Drill clearance holes for the wing and tail pegs g and h to take 6mm ($\frac{1}{4}$in) dowels. Drill pilot holes for No. 6 screws at b and d.

Cut from 4mm ($\frac{1}{6}$in) plywood

Cut out the body, beak, wing and tail. Cut out the interiors of the Owl's body. Drill 6mm ($\frac{1}{4}$in) clearance holes for the wing and tail pegs g and h. Cut a shallow channel on the underside linking g and h to take a length of string.

Drill 6mm ($\frac{1}{4}$in) holes in the wing and tail at G and H. Weight the inside upper edge of the wing with lead fishing tackle, flattened by a mole wrench. The legs will be cut out with the claws, as described below.

Cut from 1.5mm ($\frac{1}{16}$in) skin (Aero) ply

To achieve perfect register, the 4mm ($\frac{1}{6}$in) ply legs must be plural cut with the skin ply claws by temporarily bonding them together. See Techniques, page 5.

Cut out a backing board the same size as the background F. Cut out levers A-D. Drill 5mm ($\frac{3}{16}$in) clearance holes for No. 6 screws in levers B and D. Drill 2mm ($\frac{3}{32}$in) clearance holes for flat-headed rivets in levers B, D and C, and tab A. Assemble the movement as shown, using flat-headed rivet joints by nipping off their heads to become wider than their holes. Screw in the movement on the reverse side of the background at b and d with No. 6 screws 6mm ($\frac{1}{4}$in) long.

Materials

Skin (Aero) Ply
210 x 100 x 1.5mm
$8\frac{1}{4}$ x 4 x $\frac{1}{16}$in

Plywood
160 x 160 x 4mm
$6\frac{1}{4}$ x $6\frac{1}{4}$ x $\frac{1}{6}$in

250 x 250 x 5mm
10 x 10 x $\frac{3}{16}$in

Dowels
300 x 6mm
12 x $\frac{1}{4}$in

Battening
900 x 12 x 6mm
36 x $\frac{1}{2}$ x $\frac{1}{4}$in

Lead weights
2 flat-headed rivets

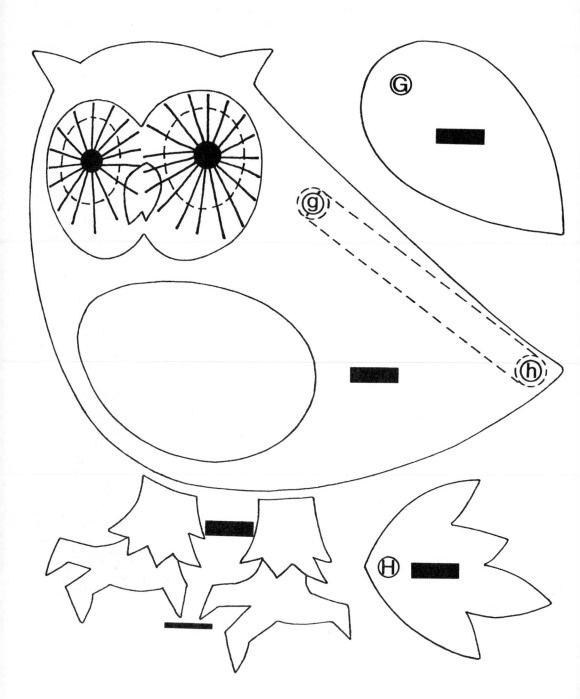

Cut from 12mm ($\frac{1}{2}$in) x 6mm ($\frac{7}{32}$in) battening
Cut out inside frame and glue and pin as indicated by dotted lines on the background F. Cut two blocks to be glued and pinned to either side of the tab A.

The blink shutter
Glue a thin piece of pink card E to the underside of the upper lever D. Draw the eyes on to white paper, extending the radiating lines beyond the eye holes. Fix the top and bottom of the paper to the background over the pink card so that it doesn't interfere with the blink shutter action. Fig. 1.

Fig. 1

The wing and tail pegs

Cut two 6mm ($\frac{1}{4}$in) dowels 16mm ($\frac{5}{8}$in) long and 12mm ($\frac{1}{2}$in) long. Drill holes for thin string, 5mm ($\frac{3}{16}$in) from the ends through each peg, drilling another small hole 2mm ($\frac{1}{16}$in) from the end of the longer peg. Insert the longer dowel peg into the wing and body at G, flush with the surface. Do likewise for the smaller dowel peg in the tail and body at H.

Insert and glue string into the tail peg H and, passing it along the channel, insert and glue it into the wing peg G. A panel pin is inserted into the peg to lock it against the underside at g.

Fig. 2

At this stage the Owl is glued to the background, thus sealing the string channel. The projecting part of the peg G has a small hole for string 2mm ($\frac{1}{16}$in) from the end. The string is knotted and threaded through, to be attached to the upright lever C.

To animate the Owl, pull out tab A which slackens the string, letting the wing drop and the tail rise. The eyes, being open, will shut and open in one pull. Push in the tab, which tightens the string raising the wing and dropping the tail. The eyes repeat the blink. Fig. 2 and 3 show the movement.

Fig. 3

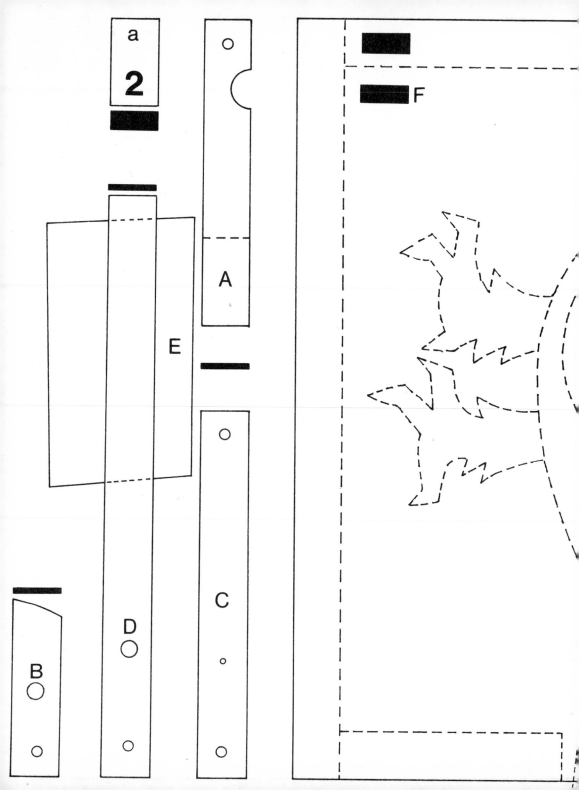

a

2

A

E

F

B

D

C

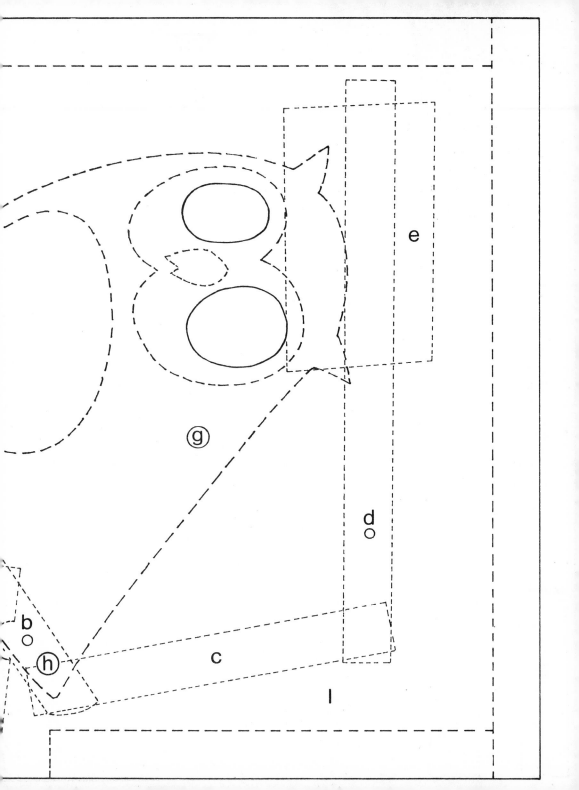

THE CLIMBING MONKEY

This is an adaptation of a 1903 tin toy. The action fascinates because the monkey really does climb up and down the string. The secret is in the double drum mechanism which enables the monkey to move up the string when it is pulled, and down when it is relaxed.

Cut from 4mm ($\frac{1}{6}$in) plywood

Cut out the two body halves and temporarily bond together. Drill four 6mm ($\frac{1}{4}$in) holes and two 2mm ($\frac{1}{16}$in) holes.

Cut out panels A, B, C, D and E. Panels A and C are double thickness and must be glued as such. Drill a hole in A, at an angle to receive the string vertically when eventually positioned, see Fig. 1. Do likewise for C. These holes can be modified later with a needle file.

Panels D and E are doors in the monkey's back. They enable you to renew the strings. Drill 2mm ($\frac{1}{16}$in) pilot holes into their sides.

Cut from 10mm ($\frac{3}{8}$in) softwood

Looks like 1/4" would be okay for arms & legs

Cut out limbs, tail and discs G and H. Drill pilot holes in lower arm and leg for No.8 screws. Drill clearance holes for No.8 screws and 6mm ($\frac{1}{4}$in) dowels in upper limbs. Drill a pilot hole for No.6 screw in the top of the tail and a clearance hole for string through the tip, the dotted lines on diagram indicate position.

Materials

Plywood
200 x 210 x 4mm
$7\frac{7}{8}$ x $8\frac{1}{4}$ x $\frac{1}{6}$in   *on hand*

Softwood
300 x 210 x 10mm
12 x $8\frac{1}{4}$ x $\frac{3}{8}$in

Dowel
410 x 6mm
16 x $\frac{1}{4}$in

4 x 3mm
$\frac{5}{16}$ x $\frac{1}{8}$in

150 x 16mm
6 x $\frac{2}{8}$in

Plastic Laminate
120 x 180 x 2mm
$4\frac{3}{4}$ x $7\frac{1}{8}$ x $\frac{1}{16}$in   *on hand*

Wire
75 x 2mm *#12 GA*
3 x $\frac{1}{16}$in   *A LITTLE BIG BUT SHOULD BE OK*

16 GA a little small

Fig. 1

50

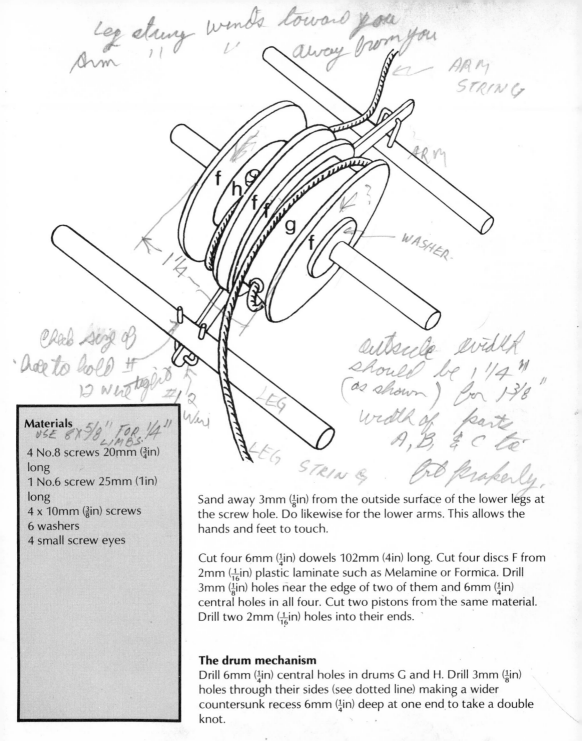

Handwritten annotations on the diagram:
- Leg string winds toward you
- Arm " " ↓ ↙ away from you
- ARM STRING
- ARM
- WASHER
- f h g f g f
- 1¼
- outside width should be 1¼" (as shown) for 1³/8" width of parts A, B, & C to fit properly.
- Check size of hole to hold it so it won't slip ½ wide
- LEG
- LEG STRING

USE 8 × ⅝" FOR ¼" LIMBS.

Materials

- 4 No.8 screws 20mm (¾in) long
- 1 No.6 screw 25mm (1in) long
- 4 x 10mm (⅜in) screws
- 6 washers
- 4 small screw eyes

Sand away 3mm (⅛in) from the outside surface of the lower legs at the screw hole. Do likewise for the lower arms. This allows the hands and feet to touch.

Cut four 6mm (¼in) dowels 102mm (4in) long. Cut four discs F from 2mm (1/16in) plastic laminate such as Melamine or Formica. Drill 3mm (⅛in) holes near the edge of two of them and 6mm (¼in) central holes in all four. Cut two pistons from the same material. Drill two 2mm (1/16in) holes into their ends.

The drum mechanism

Drill 6mm (¼in) central holes in drums G and H. Drill 3mm (⅛in) holes through their sides (see dotted line) making a wider countersunk recess 6mm (¼in) deep at one end to take a double knot.

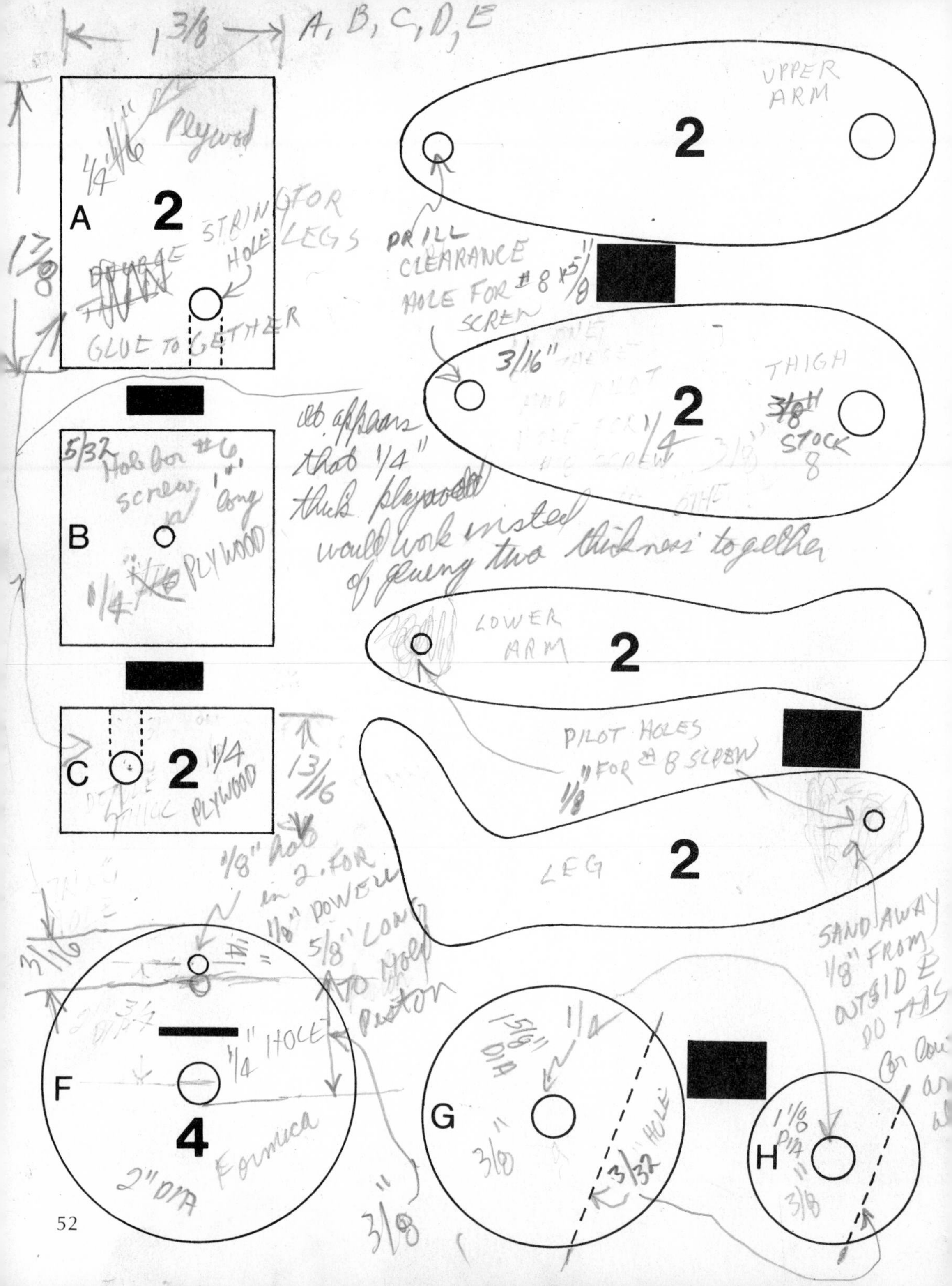

1 3/8 → A, B, C, D, E

1/4"16 Plywood

A 2
STRING FOR LEGS
HOLE
GLUE TOGETHER

5/32 Hole for #6 screw 1" long
B 2
1/4" x 16 PLYWOOD

C 2 1/4 PLYWOOD
1 3/16

UPPER ARM
2

DRILL CLEARANCE HOLE FOR #8 x 5/8" SCREW

3/16" THIGH
2 3/8 STOCK
1/4 8

it appears that 1/4" thick plywood would work insted of gluing two thickness' together

LOWER ARM 2

PILOT HOLES FOR #8 SCREW
1/8"

LEG 2

1/8" hole in 2. FOR 1/8" DOWELL 5/8" LONG TO HOLD Piston

3/16
1/4 =
1/4" HOLE
F 4
2" DIA
Formica

1 5/8" DIA
1/4
G 3/8
3/32 HOLE
3/8

SAND AWAY 1/8" FROM OUTSIDE E DO THIS

1 1/8 DIA
H 3/8

52

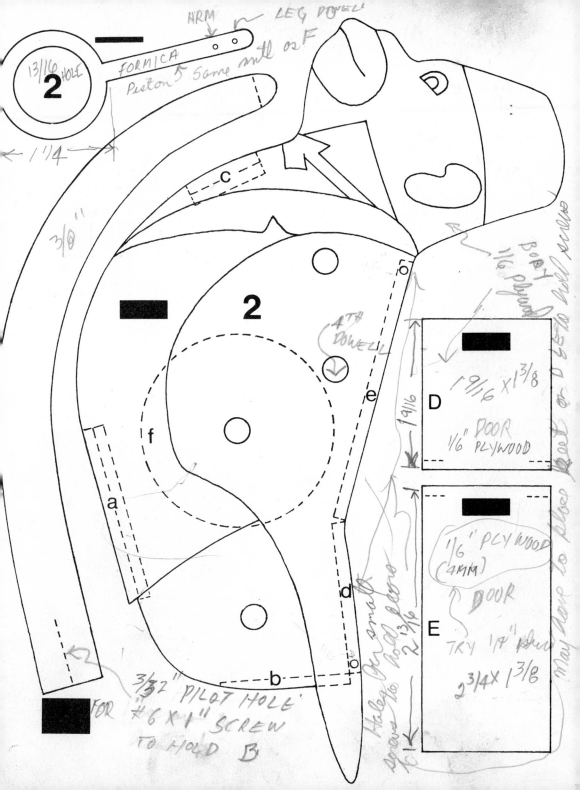

ARM   LEG DOWEL

FORMICA
Piston 5 Same mtl as F

13/16 HOLE

2

← 1¼ →

3/8"

c

4TH
DOWELL

2

e

f

a

d

b

3/32" PILOT HOLE
FOR #6 X 1" SCREW
TO HOLD B

BODY
1/6 Plywood

Roof or D ? to hold screw

May have to plane to place

D

1 9/16 X 1 3/8

DOOR
1/6" PLYWOOD

E

1/6" PLYWOOD
(4MM)

DOOR

TRY 1/4" plwd

2 3/4 X 1 3/8

Holes for small
dowel to hold door
2 13/16
TO 16

Assemble the mechanism as in the drawing. Glue the four discs F, two to each drum. Glue and pin the drums to one of the dowels. Ensure that 3mm ($\frac{1}{8}$in) dowel 8mm ($\frac{5}{16}$in) long is inserted into and between the two central discs. The two pistons hang upon the central dowel and this dowel which acts eccentrically when turned.

Drill through the arm and leg dowels to receive centrally two 2mm ($\frac{1}{16}$in) wire ends, 10mm ($\frac{3}{8}$in) apart. Bend the wires into U shapes. Insert them through the small holes in the piston ends and through the dowels. The outer hole is for the leg dowel and the inner hole for the arm dowel. Need to be at least 3/8"

Attach two 600mm (24in) lengths of string to each drum, pulling a double knot into each recess. The leg string winds towards you. The arm string away from you. Place two washers next to the outer discs. ?

Place the mechanism between the body sides fitting the dowels through their respective holes. Ensure that the lower piston is in front of the leg dowel, nearest the doors. The upper piston must be behind the arm dowel, nearest the chest. The fourth dowel keeps the string on the drum and adds support, Fig. 2 and 3.

Fig. 2

Fix B to the tail with a No.6 screw 25mm (1in) long. Glue and pin A, B and C into position. Cut plywood strips 35mm (1⅜in) wide to varying lengths from 6mm–12mm (¼in–½in). Glue into position following the monkey's outline. Fill in all gaps with plastic wood.

Fix lower and upper doors D and E with miniature 10mm (⅜in) long screws. Glue 3mm (⅛in) strips to the inside to act as door stops.

Prime with white emulsion. Paint and lacquer the monkey.

Push the strings through the holes in A and C. Put washers on the protruding arm and leg dowels. Assemble the upper and lower limbs by using No.8 screws, 20mm (¾in) long, allowing plenty of play between the joints. Screw small picture hooks into the hands and feet to take the strings. Pass the lower string through the tail. cut two 16mm (⅝in) dowels 75mm (3in) long. Drill holes through them to take the strings, and tie knots, Fig. 4.

Now test the mechanism and make adjustments. Once you are satisfied, glue and pin the upper arm and leg to their dowels. Place a protective card with a 6mm (¼in) hole over the rods and saw off the ends. Sand flat and paint the bare wood.

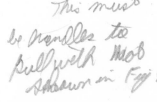

Fig. 3

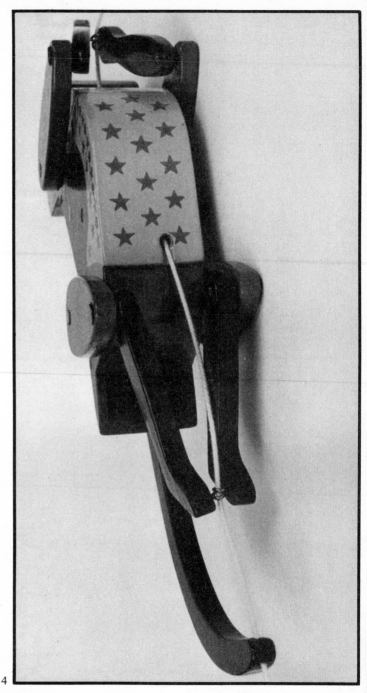

Fig. 4

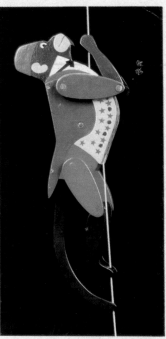

Centre) Musical Clown Bell
Toy (detail)

Bottom) The Blinking Owl

Right) The Climbing Monkey

(Top Left) Carousel
(Above) Circus Lion Pull Toy
(Left) Strong Man

MUSICAL CLOWN BELL TOY

As I mentioned in the introduction, this toy is based on a simple French automaton called *Le Clown Orchestre*. Each finger-pedal motivates a part of the clown's body, to the accompaniment of various bells.

Materials

Softwood
520 x 95 x 10mm
20 x 3¾ x ⅜in

Plywood
155 x 255 x 4mm
6 x 10 x ⅙in

Battening
675 x 12 x 5mm
26 x ½ x 3⁄16in

Piano Wire
170 x 2mm
6½ x 1⁄16in

2 pop rivet pins
4 rivet heads
10 washers
5 bells of assorted sizes
5 small screw eyes

Cut from 10mm (⅜in) softwood out of 95mm (3¾in) plank
Cut out clown pieces and pedal supports. Cut a 153mm x 95mm (6in x 3¾in) base-board. Drill 3mm (⅛in) clearance holes through the limbs, head and body. Drill 2mm (1⁄16in) holes into the edge of the cap, toes and hands as indicated by the dotted lines. Partially drill 2mm (1⁄16in) holes 5mm (3⁄16in) deep into the two pedal supports.

Cut away one third of each body half, the area indicated by the dotted line, leaving 3mm (⅛in) thickness on the outside shoulder of each half. Stick the two halves together permanently.

Fit the neck into the cavity, positioning it between two washers on a pop rivet pin 45mm (1¾in) long, see page 10. Build up the cavity, if necessary, with plastic wood, ensuring that the neck can move back and forth on the pin.

Cut from 4mm (⅙in) plywood
Cut out the remaining pieces. Drill a 3mm (⅛in) clearance hole in A. Temporarily bond the two side supports of the seat G together, and drill a 2mm (1⁄16in) hole. Separate and then glue A, B and F between side supports G. Complete by adding C, D and E.

Glue 2mm (1⁄16in) piano wire 83 mm (3¼in) long between side supports G. Fill gaps between A, B and F with plastic wood. Sand the top of the seat to a smooth curve.

Cut five finger-pedals from battens 12mm (½in) wide x 5mm (3⁄16in) thick. Drill 2mm (1⁄16in) holes through the ends of each. Drill 2mm (1⁄16) holes through the sides at the dotted line.

Before painting, place the seat on the base-board, marking its position with a pencil. Do likewise for the pedal supports.

Sand and prime with white emulsion, leaving unpainted the bottom edges of G and D, the pedal supports and the areas where they stick to the base-board. Paint in colour and decorate with sticky stars and circles. Lacquer thoroughly.

Thread and secure with a knot below, 200mm (8in) lengths of string through each finger-pedal. Assemble the pedals on 2mm ($\frac{1}{16}$in) piano wire 83mm ($3\frac{1}{4}$in) long with a washer between each pedal. The wire fits into the pedal supports which are now glued to the base-board.

Drill a pilot hole at the bottom of the torso. Screw into it through the clearance hole in A, fixing it to the seat. Stick down a thin strip 70mm ($2\frac{3}{4}$in) long on the base-board for the ends of the pedals to rest on. Glue the seat to the base-board, ensuring that the strings from the pedals pass under the wire.

Assemble the arms and head to the torso with four washers on a 45mm ($1\frac{3}{4}$in) pop rivet pin with two inverted rivet heads to act as stops. Pinch the ends to lock the pins. Assemble the legs and torso in the same way with two washers between.

Attach the various bells to the moving parts with thread knotted behind. Screw tiny screw eyes into the tops of the arms and legs and the back of the neck. Tie the pedal strings to each eye and the clown is ready to perform.

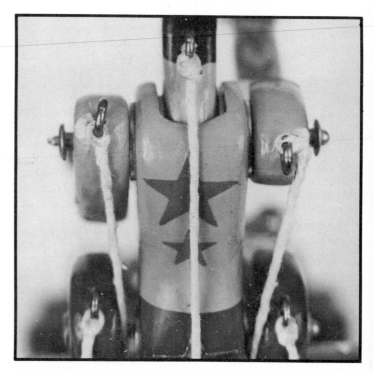

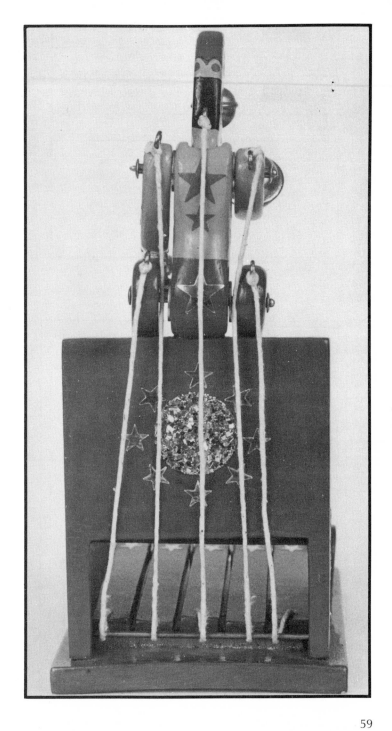

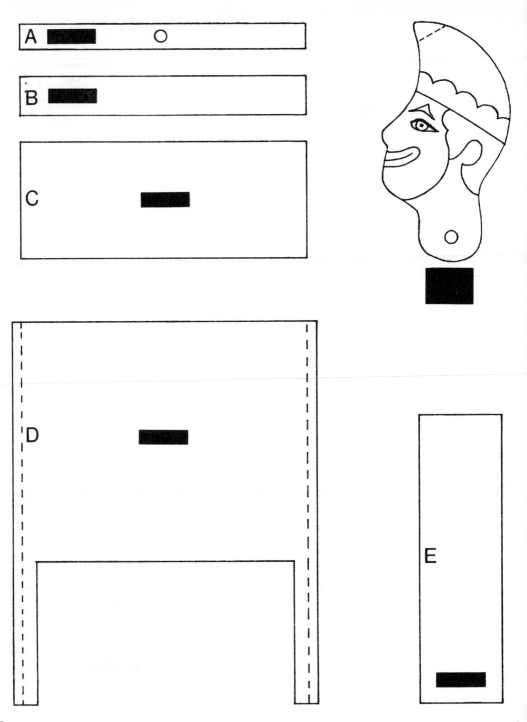

A

B

C

D

E

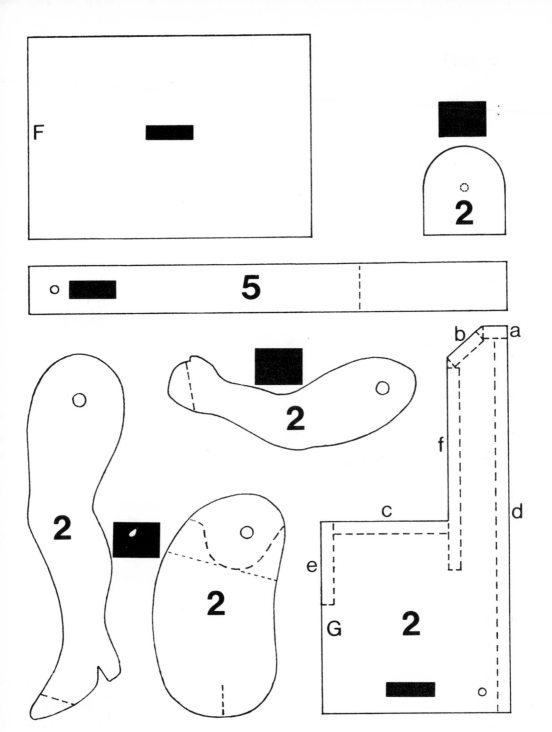

CIRCUS LION PULL-TOY

This lion wags his tail, shakes his head and rolls his eyes when pulled or pushed along. He is based on an illustration from one of my own picture books, but the mechanism, like the Drummer's, is taken from Edlin dolls of the early 19th century. You may know it better as the crankshaft principle.

Cut from 10mm ($\frac{3}{8}$in) softwood

Cut out base-board, lion bodies, wheels, wheel supports and tail support. Drill nine 6mm ($\frac{1}{4}$in) holes to a depth of 6mm ($\frac{1}{4}$in) around the base J and one through pull tab. Drill six 5mm ($\frac{3}{16}$in) holes through the centre of J. Drill four 2mm ($\frac{1}{16}$in) pilot holes in the feet of body pieces D and E along dotted line. Drill 6mm ($\frac{1}{4}$in) hole through D. Drill 2mm ($\frac{1}{16}$in) pilot hole on the reverse of E. Drill a

Fig. 1

Materials

Softwood
210 x 310 x 10mm
$8\frac{1}{4}$ x $12\frac{1}{4}$ x $\frac{3}{8}$in

Plywood
220 x 280 x 4mm
$8\frac{3}{4}$ x 11 x $\frac{1}{6}$in

Skin (Aero) Ply
100 x 100 x 2mm
4 x 4 x $\frac{1}{16}$in

Dowel
1810 x 6mm
71 x $\frac{1}{4}$in

150 x 3mm
$5\frac{3}{4}$ x $\frac{1}{8}$in

140 x 25mm
$5\frac{1}{2}$ x 1in

2 small screw eyes
1 washer with 6mm ($\frac{1}{4}$in)
central hole
lead weights
2 small black beads

central clearance hole through the tail support A and another two holes through the sides to hold the tail. Glue together the two body sections, facing right, D in front of E. Drill four 6mm ($\frac{1}{4}$in) holes in the wheel supports F.

Cut from 4mm ($\frac{1}{6}$in) plywood
Cut out the back panel 160mm x 175mm (6$\frac{1}{8}$in x 6$\frac{7}{8}$in). Cut out the two manes, G and temporarily bond together. Drill 6mm ($\frac{1}{4}$in) hole and prize apart. Cut out the face outline from one head and glue 2mm ($\frac{1}{16}$in) skin ply H into position behind.

Cut out the face features from the outline and glue into position on H. The eye rings must be drilled, fretted and filed. Enclose small black beads and cover with acetate or transparent film, shaped to fit and glued in position, Fig.1.

Cut out headboard I, and frame K. Drill 6mm ($\frac{1}{4}$in) holes in K. Cut out four wheel caps B. Paint all parts before fixing where necessary.

Fig. 2

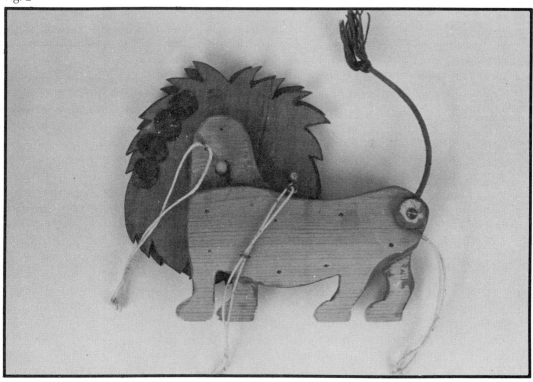

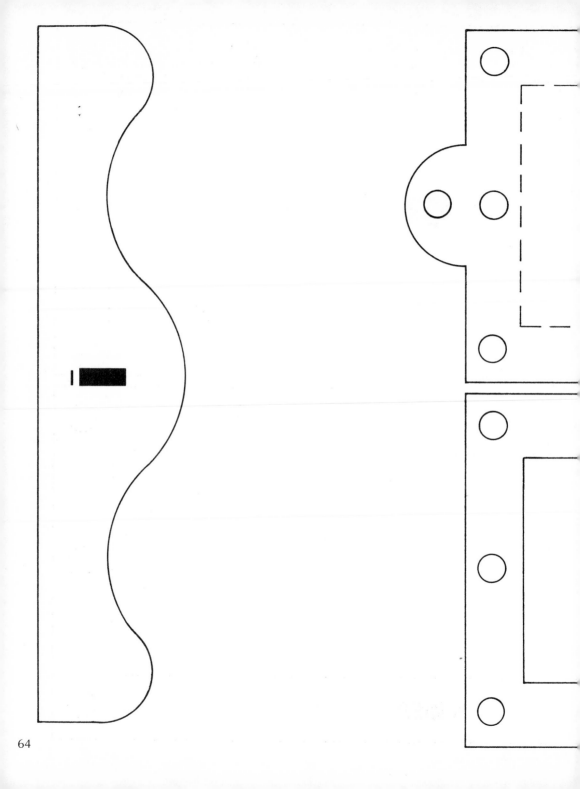

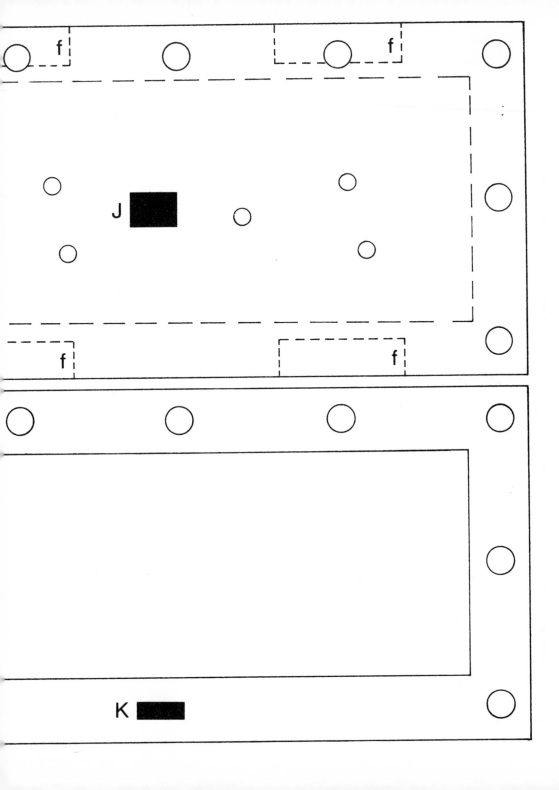

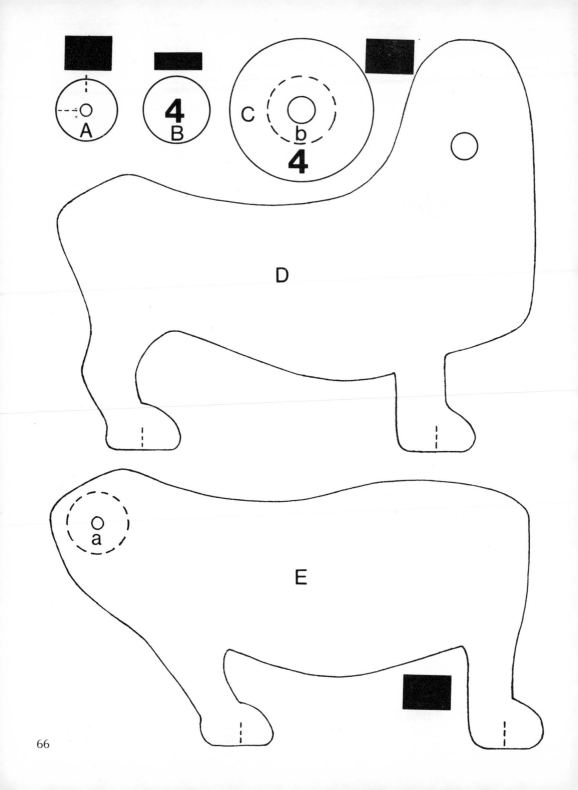

A

4
B

C
b
4

D

O
a
E

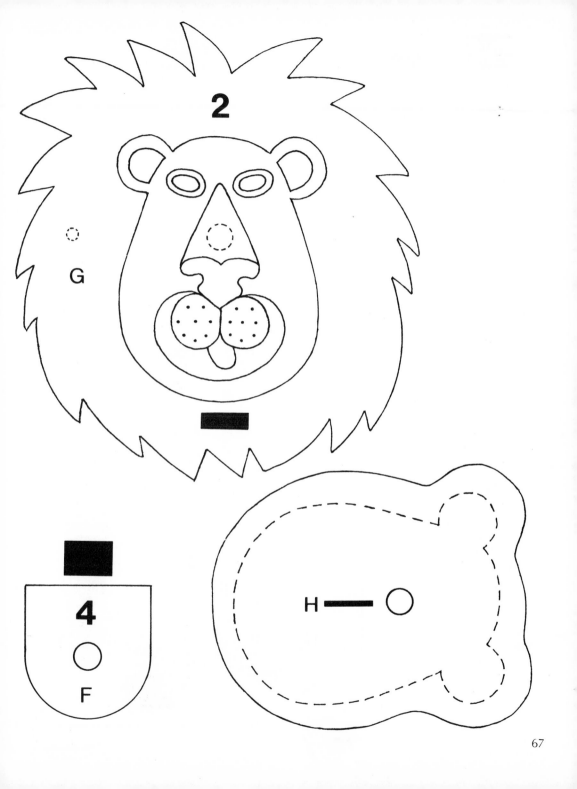

2

G

4

F

H━━○

Lion

Cut 6mm ($\frac{1}{4}$in) dowel 38mm ($1\frac{1}{2}$in) long. Drill 3mm ($\frac{1}{8}$) hole 3mm ($\frac{1}{8}$in) from the end and 2mm ($\frac{1}{16}$in) hole 14mm ($\frac{9}{16}$in) from the end. Glue and insert 6mm ($\frac{1}{4}$in) dowel flush with the nose. Flatten some lead fishing tackle, distributing it around the back of the two halves of the mane. From the front, the outer half is weighted on the left, and the inner on the right. Drill 3mm ($\frac{1}{8}$in) hole in the inner half to the left, indicated with a dotted circle. Place a washer on the central dowel between the two halves.

Insert the 6mm ($\frac{1}{4}$in) dowel through the hole in D ensuring easy clearance. Insert a piece of wire through 2mm ($\frac{1}{16}$in) hole locking G and H to the back of D. Insert 3mm ($\frac{1}{8}$in) dowel 25mm (1in) long

Fig. 3

Fig. 5

into the end hole of 6mm ($\frac{1}{4}$in) dowel. Fix a small screw eye 6mm ($\frac{1}{4}$in) from the end, pointing downwards. Cut 3mm ($\frac{1}{8}$in) dowel 32mm (1$\frac{1}{4}$in) long. Insert and glue flush with the back of the inner mane. Fix a small screw eye as before.

Fix 90mm (3$\frac{1}{2}$in) length of cotton covered elastic into the side hole in A. Tie on a string knot and fray out the ends of the tail. Trim. Glue and pin a 240mm (8in) piece of string to the top of A. See Fig. 2.

Cage

Cut nine 6mm ($\frac{1}{4}$in) dowels to 180mm (7in) lengths. Leave 6mm ($\frac{1}{4}$in) of the ends unpainted. Insert the dowels into the painted base J. Glue the back panel into position against the rear two bars. Pass frame K over the bars and parallel to the base, resting on the back panel. Slightly flatten the front edges of the projecting 10mm ($\frac{3}{8}$in) of the bars. Glue the headboard I against them and the frame, Fig. 3.

Wheels and axle

Cut 25mm (1in) dowel into two 42mm (1$\frac{5}{8}$in) lengths, and two 16mm ($\frac{5}{8}$in) lengths. Drill central 6mm ($\frac{1}{4}$in) holes to a depth of 16mm ($\frac{5}{8}$in) for the former and right through the latter. Drill two further 3mm ($\frac{1}{8}$in) holes off-centre in the undrilled ends of the longer 25mm (1in) dowel and in a corresponding position in one end of the shorter 25mm (1in) dowel. Cut two 3mm ($\frac{1}{8}$in) dowels 45mm (1$\frac{3}{4}$in) long. Insert and glue in the off-centre holes so that the two dowels are 12mm ($\frac{1}{2}$in) apart, Fig. 4.

Fig. 4

Cut four 38mm (1½in) lengths from 6mm (¼in) dowels. Insert and glue them flush with the wheels C. Glue on the wheel caps B, Fig. 5. Glue the wheel supports F to the underside of the base J. Screw the lion's feet to the base through the clearance holes for No. 8 screws 20mm (¾in) long. Insert the wheel dowels through the supports, into the axles and glue.

The string mechanism

Feed two 240mm (8in) lengths of string through the hooks in the 3mm (⅛in) dowels. Pass the string through the holes in the base J. Temporarily tie them to the front axle 3mm (⅛in) dowel. Take the two ends of string attached to tail support A and pass them through the base hole. Tie them to the back axle dowel.

The tail moves up and down and the mane halves shake in opposite directions, rolling the eyes when the toy is pulled along. Test the movements by experimenting with loop lengths. Tie and glue the knot when you've got it right.

MODELS

DOUBLE HEADED STRONGMAN

This is a shelf piece masquerading as a toy; or perhaps it's the other way about. The dumb-bell head is a surrealist notion used by the painter Magritte. I have merely animated it by turning the bar at the wrist, presenting an alternative head. The design is not Magritte's, needless to say.

Cut from 10mm ($\frac{3}{8}$in) softwood

Cut out the body, hand and base-board. Drill two pilot holes into the base of the feet to take No. 8 screws 25mm (1in) long. Cut below the wrist.

Cut a base-board 65mm x 145mm ($2\frac{5}{8}$in x $5\frac{3}{4}$in). Drill two clearance holes 50mm (2in) apart, centred along the board. Countersink the underside. Drill a 2mm ($\frac{1}{16}$in) hole to a depth of 16mm ($\frac{5}{8}$in) towards the elbow. Scrape some pencil lead shavings into the hole. Place the hand piece in position, over it. Invert, and the lead shavings will fall exactly where you must drill a matching 2mm ($\frac{1}{16}$in) hole into the wrist. Drill a horizontal 5mm ($\frac{3}{16}$in) hole through the hand to take the 75mm (3in) long dowel.

Materials

Softwood
160 x 260 x 10mm
$6\frac{1}{4}$ x $10\frac{1}{4}$ x $\frac{3}{8}$in

Dowel
75 x 3mm
3 x $\frac{1}{8}$in

2 x 35mm ($1\frac{3}{8}$in) wooden balls

short length 2mm ($\frac{1}{16}$in) piano wire

2 No. 8 screws 25mm (1in) long

Cut 2mm ($\frac{1}{16}$in) piano wire 32mm (1$\frac{1}{4}$in) long. Glue it into the arm hole.

You need two 35mm (1$\frac{3}{8}$in) wooden balls for the dumb-bell heads. They must be drilled with 10mm ($\frac{3}{8}$in) holes to a depth of 20mm ($\frac{3}{4}$in) to receive 3mm ($\frac{1}{8}$in) dowel 75mm (3in) long.

When fitting the wrist with the dumb-bell in position, ensure that the heads just brush the neck, momentarily locking into place.

Paint and decorate with self-stick stars and circles. Fix the Strongman to the base-board with No. 8 screws 25mm (1in) long into the feet.

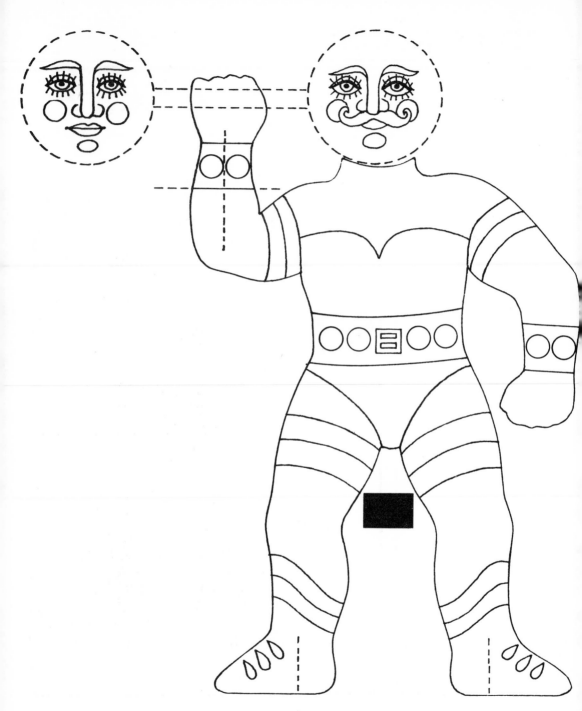

NOAH'S ARK

This Noah's Ark is designed with a surprise and a puzzle. It owes little to antique toy arks, beyond the device of painting a dove on the roof, holding an olive branch to show the abating of the flood. The surprise is concealed and contained between decks: a build-it-yourself rainbow. The puzzle is to fit the animals and Mr and Mrs Noah neatly into the box. This is easily done and explained in the text and pictures.

Materials

Plywood
380 x 305 x 4mm
15 x 12 x $\frac{1}{6}$in

Softwood
610 x 230 x 10mm
24 x 9 x $\frac{3}{8}$in

Dowel
258 x 5mm
$10\frac{1}{4}$ x $\frac{3}{16}$in

65 x 8mm
$2\frac{1}{2}$ x $\frac{5}{16}$in

22 x 16mm
$\frac{7}{8}$ x $\frac{5}{8}$in

adhesive pvc sheeting

Cut from 4mm ($\frac{1}{6}$in) plywood
Cut out ark house pieces B-E. Drill twelve 15mm ($\frac{9}{16}$in) holes, using a hole saw bit, through D. Drill six holes, likewise, through E, and two more through B. All these are duplicated, being the four sides of the cabin, enclosing an inner box for the animals.

Cut out a rectangle from the roof F. Glue the shutters G into position on either side. Cut out the rudder H and tiller support A.

Glue the inner box side pieces E to end pieces C. Glue the cabin sides D to end B. Glue the roof F to ends B. Cut a 5mm ($\frac{3}{16}$in) dowel 220mm ($8\frac{11}{16}$in) long and glue it to the apex of the roof.

Cut from 10mm ($\frac{3}{8}$in) softwood
Cut out the two hulls and top deck. Drill 8mm ($\frac{5}{16}$in) hole through the top deck 1 at a. Drill 8mm ($\frac{5}{16}$in) hole in the underside of the bow to a depth of 5mm ($\frac{3}{16}$in).

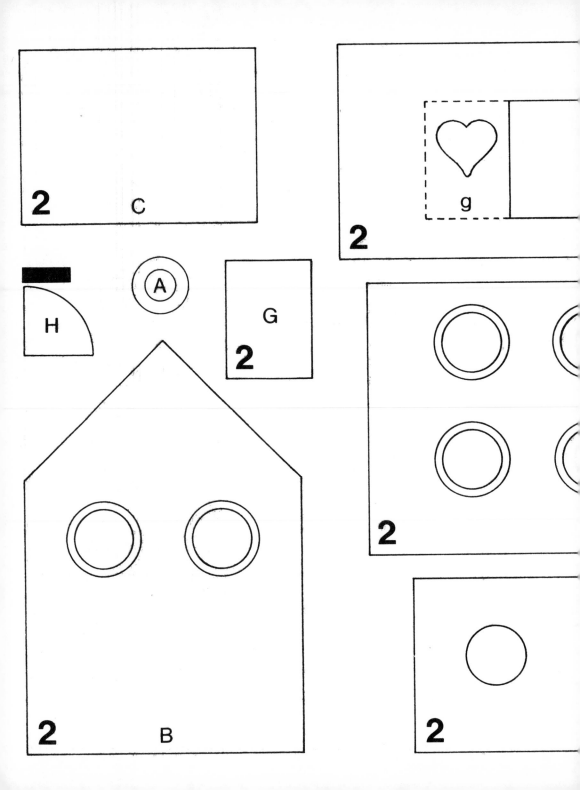

2 C

2 g

2 G

2

A

H

2 B

2

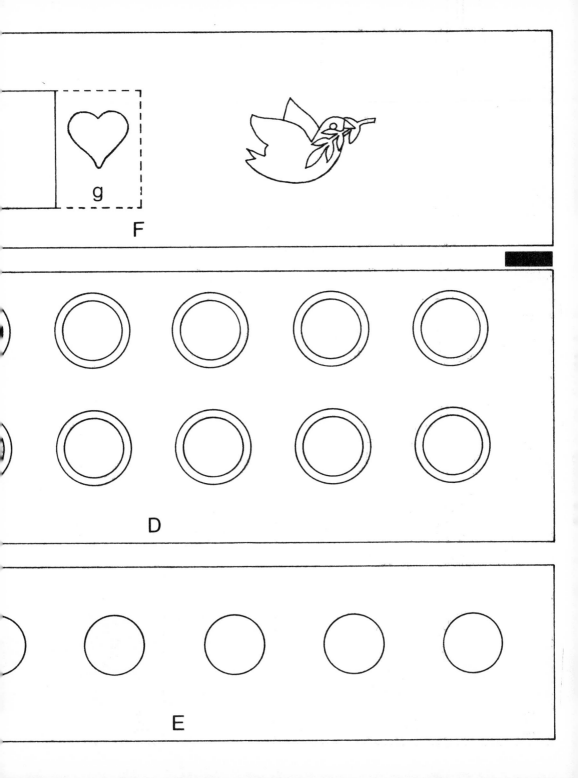

F

D

E

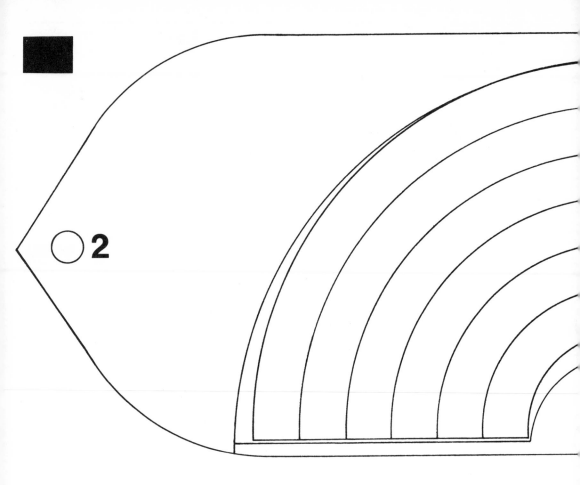

○ **2**

J

K

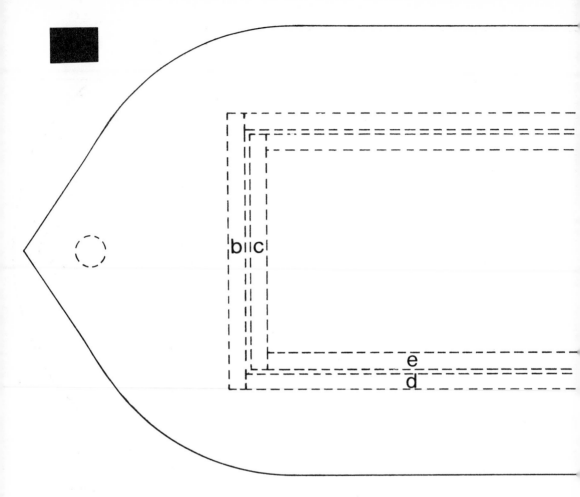

Drill 8mm ($\frac{5}{16}$in) holes through the two thicknesses of the hull J to register with the holes in the deck 1. Cut a semi-circle from the upper part of the hull. Cut out the rainbow support K and glue in position on the hull.

Cut out the rainbow in six pieces. Tape them together and saw across their bases so that they pack solid when standing on end. There should of course be seven colours but as this is not a scientific model we claim artistic licence! Colour the pieces from the outside to the centre: red, orange, yellow, green, blue and purple.

Cut an 8mm ($\frac{5}{16}$in) dowel 65mm (2$\frac{1}{2}$in) long. Drill 5mm ($\frac{3}{16}$in) hole, 16mm ($\frac{5}{8}$in) from its end. Insert 5mm ($\frac{3}{16}$in) dowel 38mm (1$\frac{1}{2}$in) long

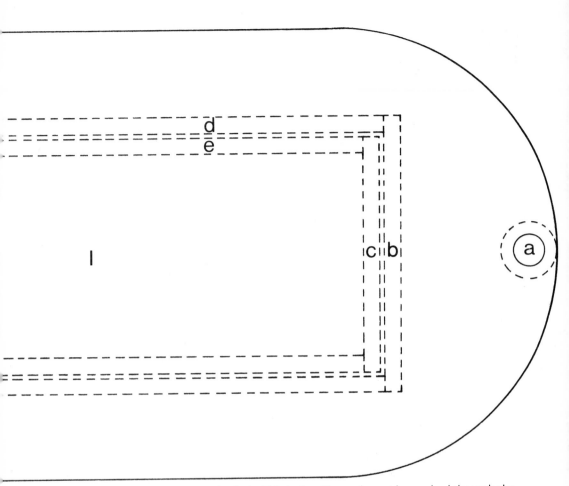

into the hole. This is the tiller and must be pushed through the
tiller support A and its hole. Glue the two parts of the hull
together. Insert the tiller at the stern and glue on the rudder.

Insert a 16mm ($\frac{5}{8}$in) dowel 22mm ($\frac{7}{8}$in) long into the bow hole so
that 3mm ($\frac{1}{8}$in) projects upwards. This will fit into the underside of
the deck, which swivels on the tiller dowel and locks on the bow
dowel. Paint the cabin and stick on white circles around the
portholes. These you can cut from adhesive pvc sheeting such as
Fablon with a compass cutter.

Glue the inner box on to the deck I, on the dotted line c and e.
The cabin fits loosely over it allowing the giraffes' necks to poke
through. Details of the animals berthing arrangements are
described later.

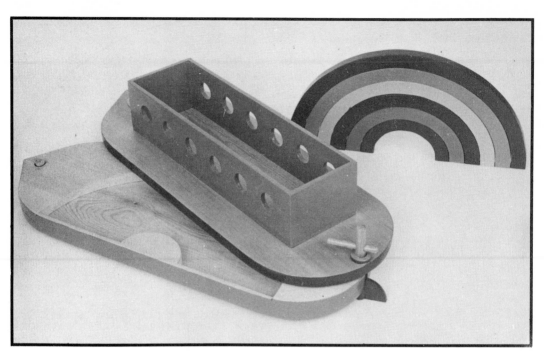

NOAH'S ANIMALS

We took artistic licence with the rainbow by reducing its colours to six, and I now propose to compound that latitude by diminishing the number of animals. If your favourites aren't here, they're on the next boat!

Cut from 10mm ($\frac{3}{8}$in) softwood
It is tempting to try to plural cut the duplicate animals, but it would be very heavy going on most fretsaws. Cut templates and draw the outlines on to wood. Ensure that all bases are flat so that the figures can stand. Don't paint them – they're better left in a natural wood state. Just lacquer.

This is how they fit into the box:
Row 1 Giraffes over tortoises, camels over mice, penguins, doves, Mr and Mrs Noah.
Row 2 Elephants, crocodiles over kangaroos.
Row 3 Rhinos, snakes over hippos.

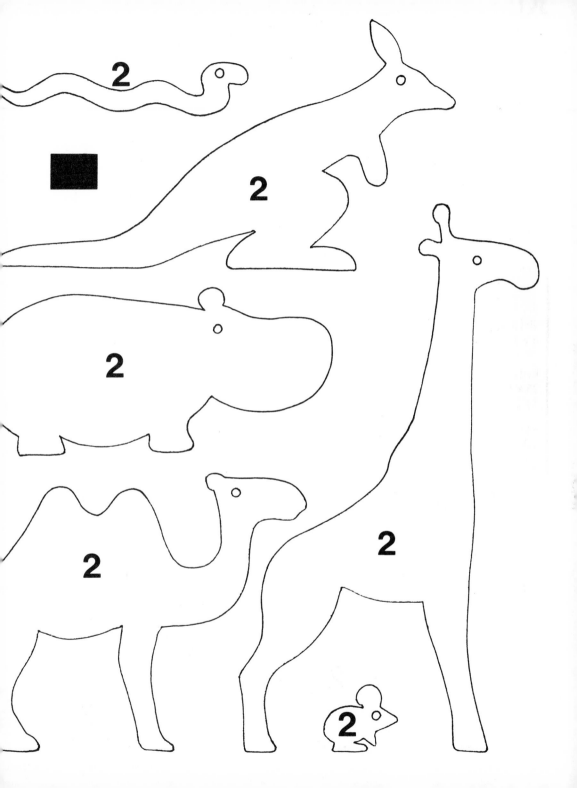

SCISSORS TOY SOLDIERS

The idea of the scissors toy goes back to the 16th century. They are sometimes called 'lazy tongs' after those used by confectioners. Very popular in Saxony, they often took the form of soldiers. My troop have completely fabricated uniforms and could belong to any army.

It's a simple but repetitive toy to make. The effect, though, is very decorative and well worth the effort. You could have ten soldiers if you have the patience to recruit them! I settled for seven.

The cutting guide gives a surface design, so you can either photocopy the soldiers or trace them, offsetting the design on to wood. If you choose the latter method you may also like to make a template of the outline for the repeat work.

Materials

Softwood
203 x 810 x 10mm
8 x 32 x $\frac{3}{8}$in

Battens (8)
25 x 3 x 125mm
1 x $\frac{1}{8}$ x 5in

7 No.6 screws 25mm (1in) long
3 No.6 screws 6mm ($\frac{1}{4}$in) long
10 washers

Cut from 10mm ($\frac{3}{8}$in) softwood
Cut out all the soldiers. Drill pilot holes into the boots for No. 6 screws 25mm (1in) long.

Cut from 25mm x 3mm (1in x $\frac{1}{8}$in) battens 125mm (5in) long
Drill ten clearance holes for No. 6 screws through the ends and centres of the bottom slats, leaving two ends undrilled. Drill six clearance holes in the ends of the top slats, leaving two ends free and one central clearance hole. Drill three central pilot holes for No. 6 screws on the undersides of the three top slats – without breaking the surface. Glue and pin the soldiers into their correct positions. To do this, temporarily fix them with their 25mm (1in) screws. Drill 1mm ($\frac{1}{32}$in) holes either side of the screws and insert fourteen panel pins. Unscrew and assemble the slats with No. 6 screws, 6mm ($\frac{1}{4}$in) long, a washer on each screw.

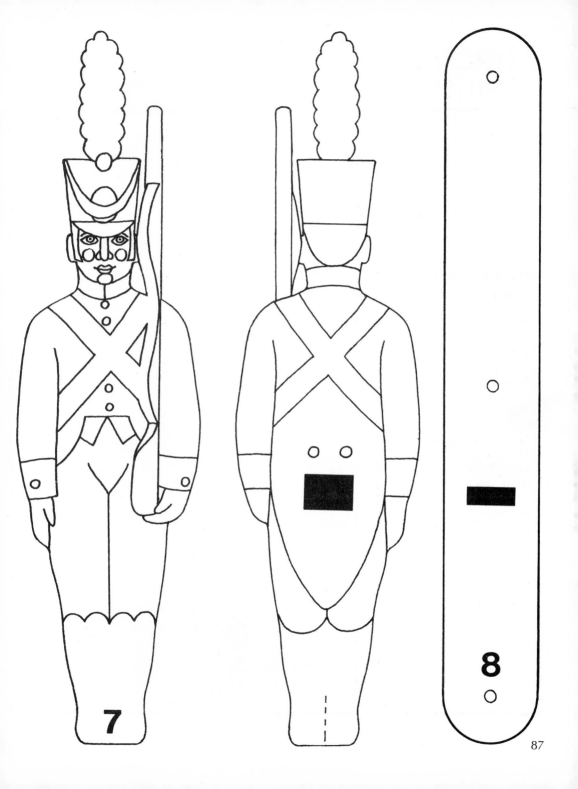

7

8

CAROUSEL BATTERY MODEL

Fig. 1

Materials

Plywood
860 x 305 x 4mm
34 x 12 x $\frac{1}{6}$in

155 x 155 x 6mm
6 x 6 x $\frac{1}{4}$in

Skin (Aero) Ply
305 x 305 x 1.5mm
12 x 12 x $\frac{1}{16}$in

Piano Wire
83 x 1mm
$3\frac{1}{4}$ x $\frac{1}{32}$in

930 x 2mm
$36\frac{3}{4}$ x $\frac{1}{16}$in

Cardboard Roll
83 x 38mm
$3\frac{1}{4}$ x $1\frac{1}{2}$in

Brass Tube
145 x 2mm
$5\frac{3}{4}$ x $\frac{1}{16}$in

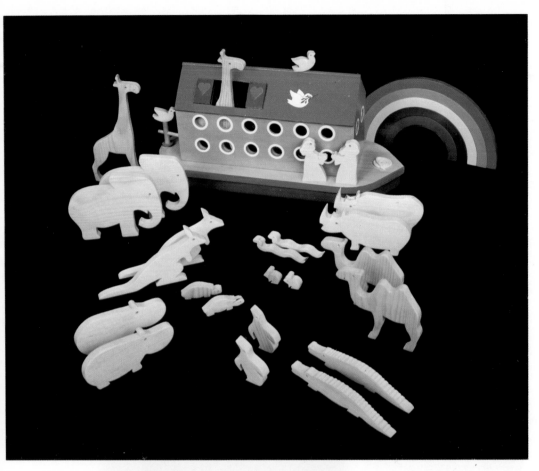

(Above) Noah's Ark

(Left) Hand-wound Drummer (left) and Musical Clown (right)

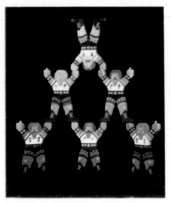

(Above) Soldiers
  Scissors Toy

(Left) Hole-and-Peg
  Acrobats

(Right) Punch and Judy
  Show

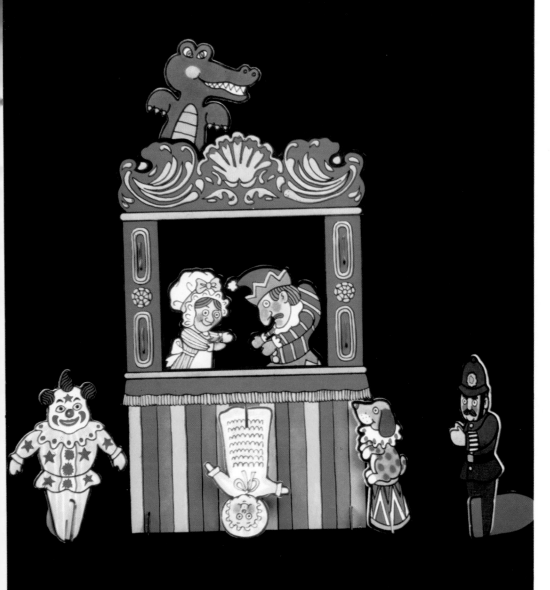

(Below) Bird Tree
(Top Right) Alphabet
(Bottom Right) Money Box

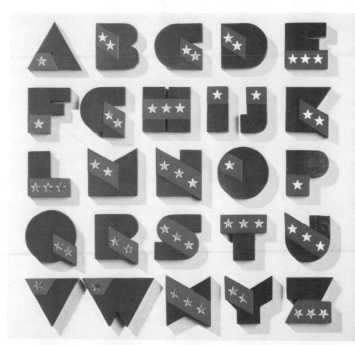

In Victorian times toy roundabouts were made with a clockwork mechanism, sometimes incorporating a musical movement. This model is driven by an electric clock motor powered by a 1.5 volt battery, running silently at two speeds. The balance wheel must be de-activated to produce a fast speed and a 6 ohm resistor installed to slow it down. Remove the hands and dial before you start.

The model bears little relation to an actual carousel, being a fanciful toy evocation of the Victorian fairground. For all that, it is a fairly elaborate model to make and we shall have to establish a working terminology for the main parts.

From the bottom up, see Fig. 1, they are: drum base – pillars – rotating disc – rotating collar – cartwheel – support blocks (for horses) – centre drum – spinning frame – platform – fascia drum – dome. Prime and paint each stage before assembly.

Cut from 4mm ($\frac{1}{6}$in) plywood

Cut out multiples of pieces B, C, D and P as indicated. Temporarily bond together three discs D. Drill six 2mm ($\frac{1}{16}$in) holes. Prize apart and cut openings in two of the discs to house the clock motor and battery. These are the top and bottom of the drum base. Drill a central 2mm ($\frac{1}{16}$in) hole into the third disc, which is the platform.

Glue thirty-six drum base side panels C between the discs D enclosing the clock mechanism. Fill in between panels with plastic

Fig. 2

Materials

Cored solder
Electric clock motor
powered by
1.5v battery
6ohm resistor pin
Small piece of tin sheet
Knobs 6 x 12mm ($\frac{1}{2}$in)

wood, sand, prime, paint and decorate. Fig. 2 shows the stages of this from left to right.

Cut two discs P. Drill 12mm ($\frac{1}{2}$in) hole for the rotating disc and 2mm ($\frac{1}{16}$in) hole for the spinning frame. Cut two rotating collars B, drilling out their centres.

Make six horses from 4mm ($\frac{1}{6}$in) plywood in the manner described for the Rocking Horse, page 12.

Pillars

Cut six pieces of 2mm ($\frac{1}{16}$in) piano wire 155mm ($6\frac{1}{8}$in) long. Wind cored solder spirally around each wire, starting 38mm ($1\frac{1}{2}$in) from the base to within 3mm ($\frac{1}{8}$in) of the top. Cover thickly with gold enamel paint. Insert and glue the 38mm ($1\frac{1}{2}$in) ends through the top and flush with the bottom of the drum base.

The clock mechanism

Having de-activated the balance wheel and dismantled the hands, you will see that the pivot governs three speeds, for the hour, minute and second hands.

The hour hand ring, which moves very slowly, is fixed to the rotating disc with plastic padding. This is then covered by one of the rotating collars B. In my model this has been done by fixing a metal piece under the collar, but this is unnecessary to the movement. The minute hand ring is left free. The second hand ring has a small piece of wire around the spindle, twisted and soldered into a projecting arm 10mm ($\frac{3}{8}$in) long, Fig. 3.

Cut from 6mm ($\frac{1}{4}$in) plywood

Cut out pieces A and E. The cartwheel A has a central arbor fitting over the wire arm. Use a cog wheel with a brass arbor and drill out enough metal to accommodate the second hand ring, making a groove to lock the wire arm. This drives the carousel.

Glue the support blocks E 8mm ($\frac{5}{16}$in) away from the spoke ends. Fix on the horses so that they spin without touching the pillars.

Glue the other rotating collar B to the centre of the cartwheel. Make the centre drum from 38mm ($1\frac{1}{2}$in) cardboard roll 83mm ($3\frac{1}{4}$in) tall. Cut 2mm ($\frac{1}{16}$in) card discs with central 2mm ($\frac{1}{16}$in) holes to fit the top and bottom of the drum and glue in place.

Fig. 3.

Fig. 4

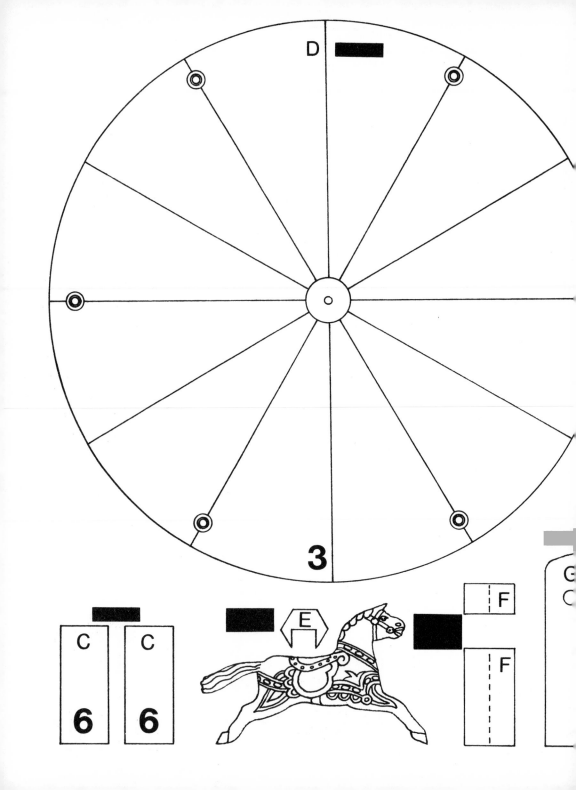

D

3

C
6

C
6

E

F

F

G

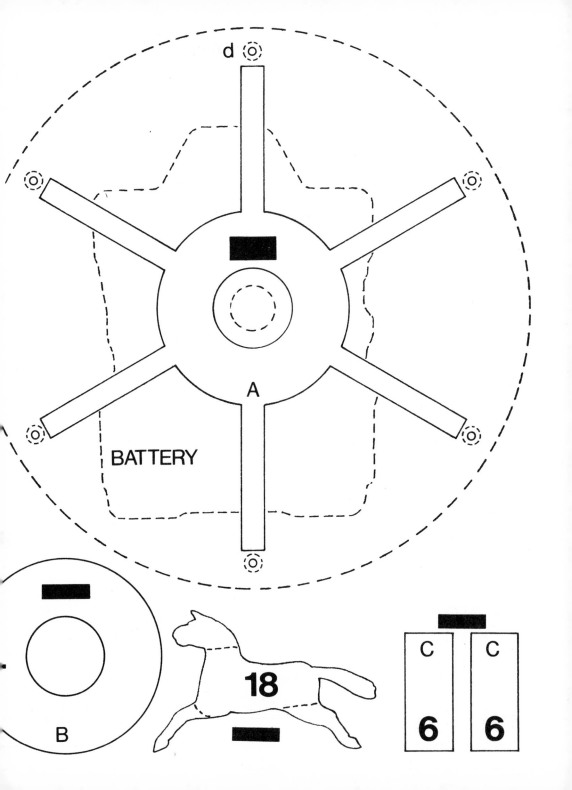

d

A

BATTERY

B

18

C   C

6   6

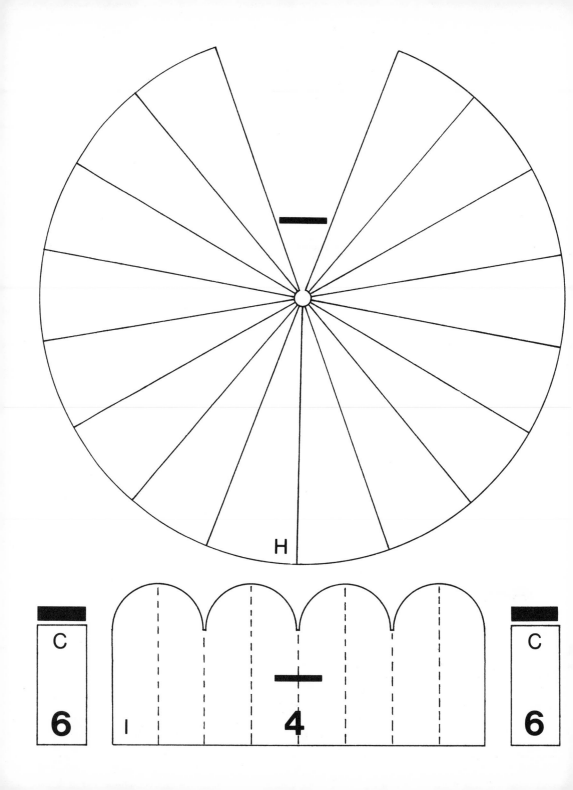

H

C

6

I

4

C

6

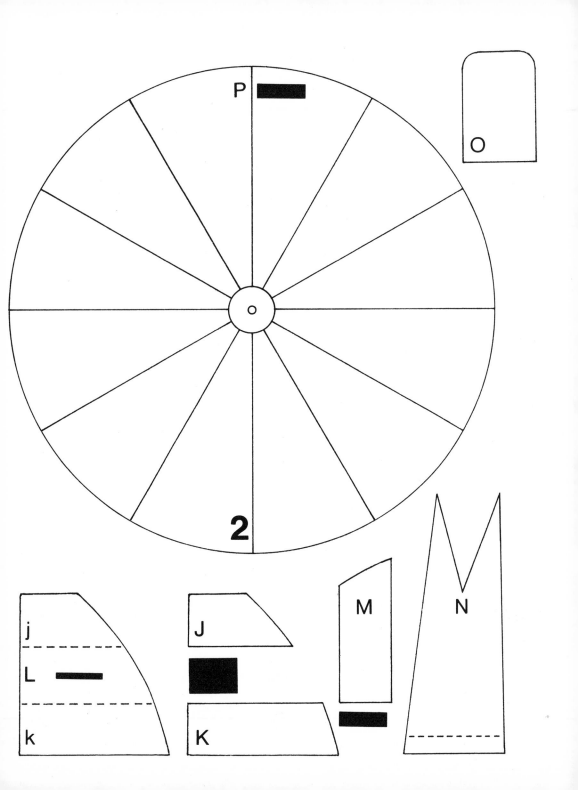

P

O

2

j
L
k

J

K

M

N

Central assembly

Glue the centre drum to the cartwheel assembly and the spinning frame to the centre drum. Pass 2mm ($\frac{1}{16}$in) brass tube 145mm ($5\frac{3}{4}$in) long through the assembly flush with the lower disc, Fig. 4 and 5. Decorate the edge of the spinning frame with 10mm ($\frac{3}{8}$in) wide metallic gold tape glued on. Fit the platform over the tube and on to the pillar tops. Cover these ends with gold spots.

Cut from 1.5mm ($\frac{1}{16}$in) skin (Aero) ply

Cut out pieces H, I and P. Score along the dotted lines of the four fascia panels I, bending them into a curve. Cut out two discs, the same size as the spinning frame P. Drill a central 2mm ($\frac{1}{16}$in) hole into them. Glue the curved fascia panels to the edges of the discs to make the fascia drum, Fill in the gaps with plastic wood, sand, prime, paint and decorate.

Using plastic padding, centrally fix a cog wheel, the arbor of which is fitted with a grub screw, to the top of the fascia drum. Raise the drum 3mm ($\frac{1}{8}$in) to clear the platform and tighten the grub screw against the brass tube.

Score along the lines of the dome H so that the sections can be split and bent into a shallow cone. Use masking tape on the underside to keep the sections together.

Cut 1mm ($\frac{1}{32}$in) piano wire 83mm ($3\frac{1}{4}$in) long. Fold and glue the paper flag N to it. The wire pole fits into the brass tube through the hole in the dome, Fig. 6.

The switching gear

Cut out pieces F, G, J, K, L, M and O, the cutting guide gives thicknesses. The underside shows the aperture for the battery and its components: the main switch G and its switch housing J, K and L; a neutralizing tin panel O covered with adhesive pvc material such as Fablon attached to its shank M; the resistor switch fixed to the resistor pin 50mm (2in) long and its housing F; and 6 ohm resistor with its wires attached to the pin and through the smaller part of F, Fig. 7.

Two wires lead from the resistor to the battery terminals. To start the motor, ensure that the resistor pin is pushed in (touching the resistor wire) and pull out the main switch. As the carousel gathers speed pull out the resistor pin (disengaging from the resistor), and the speed will drop so that the horses can be seen as more than a blur.

Attach four 12mm ($\frac{1}{2}$in) knobs to the base for feet allowing the switch gear to clear the table. The main switch and resistor pin have two knobs for handles and the former is tied with gold cord to one of the feet to prevent loss.

Fig. 6

Fig. 7

Fig. 5

PUNCH AND JUDY SHOW

Punch and Judy is probably the most popular folk play in the English language. This is not the book to trace its history or even its theme. Suffice it to say that the story is well-known enough, in conjunction with the characters represented here, to afford a child some amusement.

The characters
Punch, Judy, Doctor, Crocodile, Joey the Clown, the Baby, Toby the dog and the Policeman.

Cut from 2mm ($\frac{1}{16}$in) card (6 sheet) or 1.5mm ($\frac{1}{16}$in) skin (Aero) ply. Either trace or photocopy the designs on to card or ply and colour before cutting out. This toy was drawn on to card with a fibre-tipped pen and coloured with spirit markers. Use watercolour if you photocopy, as the paper will not take spirit markers well.

4

103

SIX HOLE-AND-PEG ACROBATS

The figures are designed so that they can slot into each other with little pegs. The pegs are interchangeable with hands and feet so that many positional permutations can be achieved. It makes an interesting rearrangeable shelf-piece.

Cut from 12mm (½in) softwood
Drill 5mm (3/16in) holes into the feet and hands as indicated by the dotted line. Cut four 5mm (3/16in) dowels 16mm (5/8in) long for each figure.

Paint and punch out coloured metallic card discs to decorate the front and sides. If you want to decorate the back, repeat the design for the front, but paint the hair in a circle and omit the button holes on the boots.

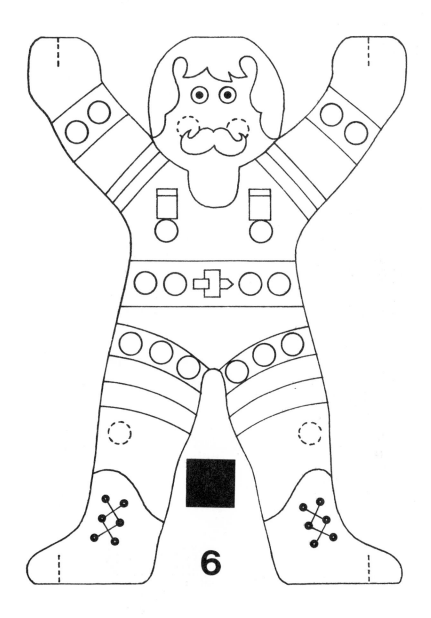

6

SLOT TOGETHER MONEY BOX

To construct this it is only necessary to cut out six modular pieces together from skin ply. You can decorate each facet with concentric circles, stick on magazine graphics, or apply your own design.

You can, if you wish, make two boxes in one by designing each facet with an alternative design on its reverse side (twelve facets in all).

Cut from 1.5mm ($\frac{1}{16}$in) skin (Aero) ply
Drill a hole for the saw blade to cut out the money slot from one piece.

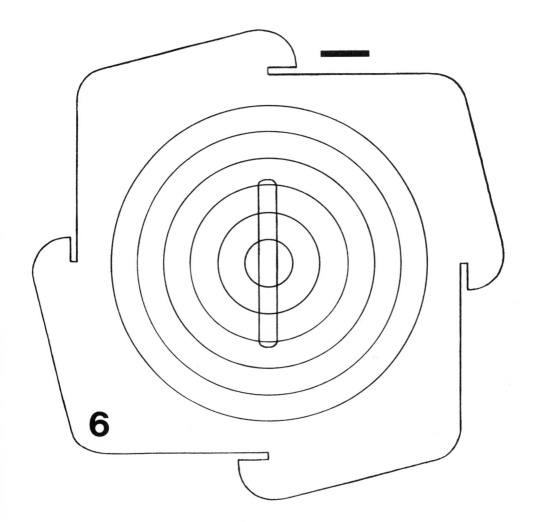

6

GOLDILOCKS AND THE THREE BEARS

The well-known fairy tale comes to life as you build up the pieces into Father Bear, Mother Bear, Baby Bear and Goldilocks. There's also a bed, a chair and a porridge plate and spoon as additional props.

Cut from 1.5mm ($\frac{1}{16}$in) skin (Aero) ply
Drill eye holes of varying sizes for Father, Mother, Baby Bear and Goldilocks. Cut the interior slots by drilling a succession of 2mm ($\frac{1}{16}$in) holes along the length of each slot. Use the drill bit as a file to break into each hole thus completing each interior slot.

Make the plate and the spoon by sticking their rims to their bases. Sand and lacquer the pieces.

Any number of characters from books and television can be made using this method.

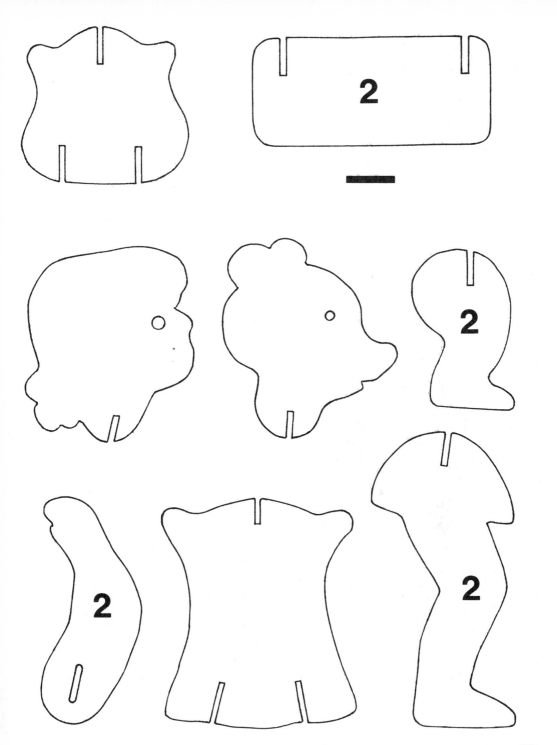

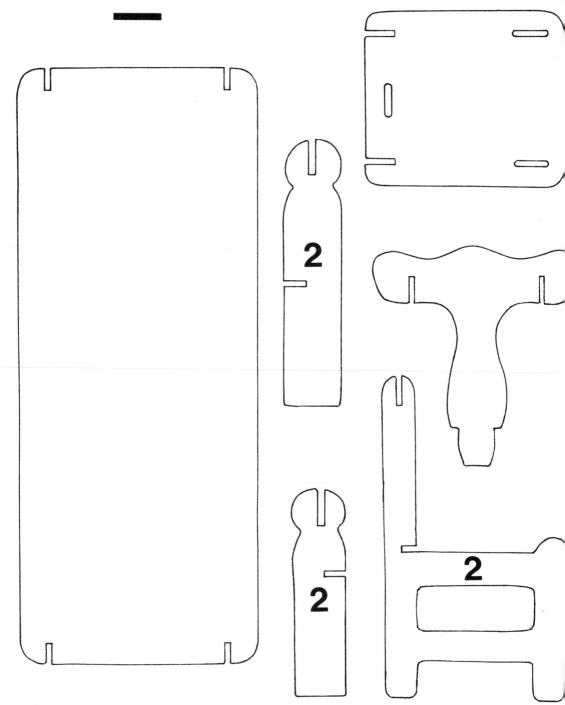

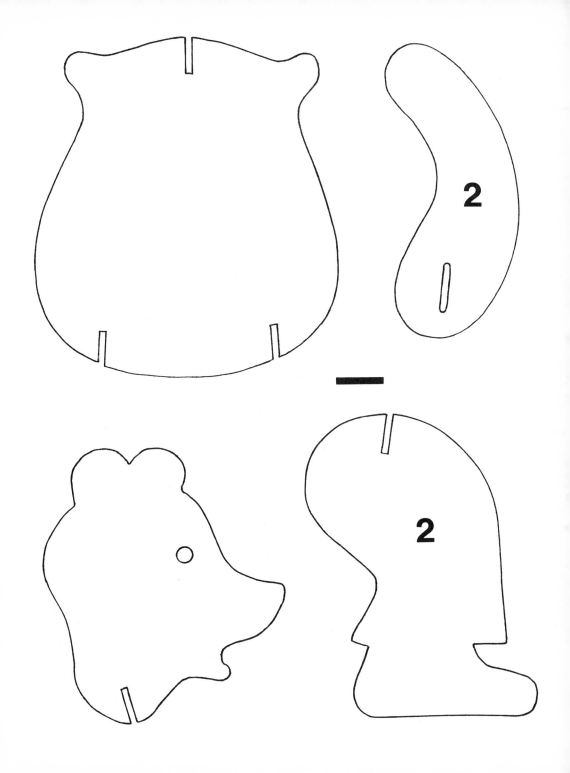

2

2

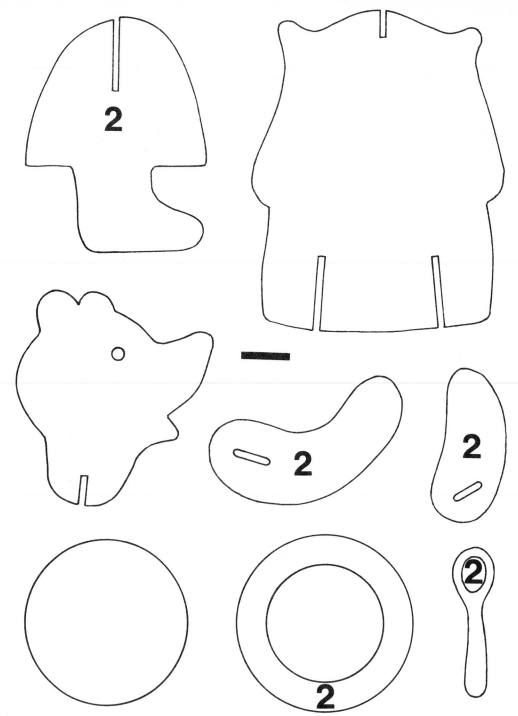

DECORATIVE TOYS

BIRD-TREE

This is based on a Japanese idea, and plays the dual role of decorative shelf-piece and puzzle. It can be arranged with all the birds in the tree; or out of the tree; or some in and some out. Ring the changes.

Cut from 10mm (⅜in) softwood
It's best to cut a card template to be sure of preserving the curves. Draw around it on to the wood.

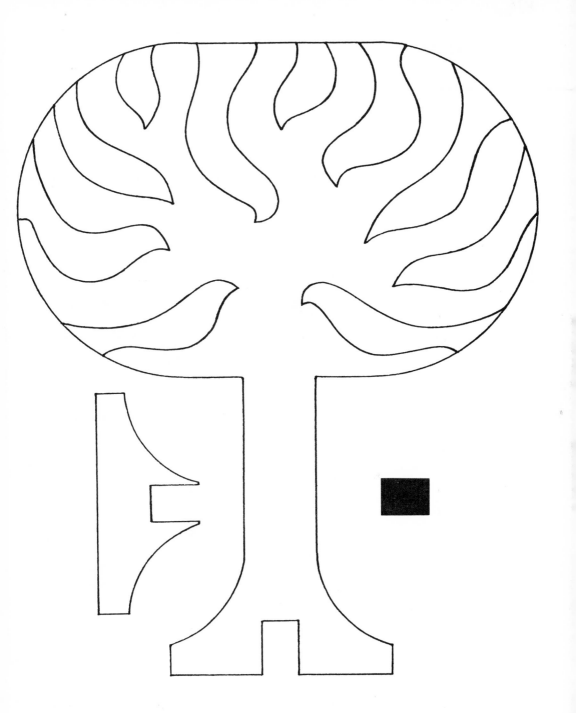

BIRDS AND WORM PUZZLE

Again, based on a Japanese idea. A very simple little puzzle for a little person – make sure he doesn't eat it!

Cut from 10mm (⅜in) softwood

Drill 2mm ($\frac{1}{16}$in) holes for the eyes and cut a curve for the worm's mouth.

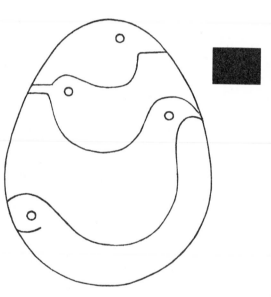

DECORATIVE ALPHABET

Based on the typeface *Sinaloa*, this alphabet is effective *en bloc* or as individual (initials) letters. It is not suitable for teaching a child the ABC, being too sophisticated for that purpose. They do make attractive and unusual building blocks.

Cut from 10mm (³⁄₈in) softwood
Lightly score straight lines with a scalpel blade to help you paint the letters. Use stick-on stars to decorate.

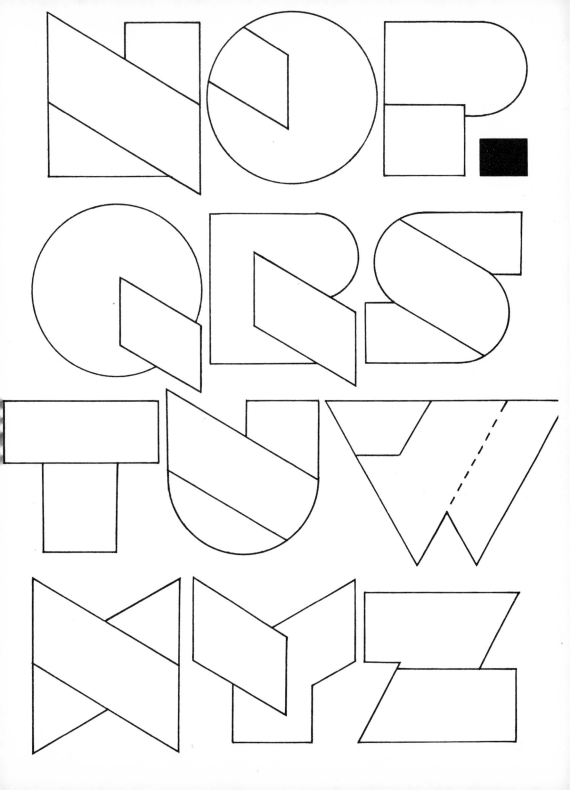